TWEETABLE LEADERSHIP

@ jim wideman

TWEETABLE LEADERSHIP

@ jim wideman

An Infuse Publication

©2015 Jim Wideman Ministries, Inc
2441Q Old Fort Parkway #354
Murfreesboro, TN 37128

www.jimwideman.com

Building Strong Leaders

"

This book is dedicated to my Timothy's in the ministry, as well as all of my wonderful Infuse coaches. Special thanks also to Clayton Poland and Jenny Funderburke, whom without their help this book would not exist. Also thank you Chris Sykes for coming up with the title. I would also like to thank my family Julie, Whitney, Yancy, Cory, and Sparrow. I love you all so much and could not do what I do without your love and support. I'm also very thankful for my Northstar and Orange families, thanks for your continued love and support!

"

CONTENTS

FORWARD

INTRODUCTION

CH. 1   #JUSTSAYING
         A LEADER IS AN EXAMPLE

CH. 2   #KIDS #FAMILY AND #PARENTING
         DEVELOPING A BIBLICAL WORLD VIEW IN YOUR CHILDREN

CH. 3   #LEADERSHIPLESSONS
         A GROWING LEADER IS A LEARNER

CH. 4   #TIMEMANAGEMENT
         KEEPING LIFE SIMPLE

CH. 5   #STRUCTURE #PLANNING AND #GROWTH
         OVERCOMING GROWTH BARRIERS

CH. 6   #VOLUNTEERS #PEOPLE AND #WISDOM
         STAYING SPIRITUALLY HEALTHY

CH. 7   #JIMISMS
         WHAT OLD JIM WISHES YOUNG JIM KNEW

Forward

For as long as I can remember, throughout my childhood and teen years, my dad talked to me. Sometimes I agreed with what he was telling me. But I'll be honest; in many of those moments, I was just going through the motions of receiving the wisdom He was passing on to me. I'm sure my eyes rolled more than once. My head nodded yes, even when I was really more interested in moving on to the next topic. But over time, I noticed a shift in my heart. In both my resistant moments and my moments spent striving to please, my ears really heard what he said. Many of his statements stuck and became standards I wanted for myself; they became bars that I set and held others to. Goals were established all because of words.

In each of those conversations, seeds were planted in my heart. Through repetition, those seeds were able to take root and be watered so that growth was cultivated. At times, one of my mindsets was changed or an attitude was adjusted. At other times, a dream was inspired and a desire to be different from the rest was encouraged. Some of the best things in life take time to develop. They don't happen overnight: they happen because someone invests time and works hard. Sacrifices are made. Rehearsals happen again and again to prepare. If you want to harvest something specific, you have to plant it first.

Proverbs 18:21 NIRV says: "Your tongue has the power of life and death. Those who love to talk will eat the fruit of their words." What you say is important. The words you speak have power in your life, your family, and your ministry.

From a young age, my parents used all conversations as teachable moments. Both when we were young children and even now as adults, they use their time talking with us to teach, guide, and challenge. It's only been in recent years that I've realized how much my dad has encouraged and still encourages me. I'm serious when I say that he doesn't end a phone call or an email without using his words to uplift me. What a gift that is.

I've heard my dad say that he didn't want to stand before the Lord and have Him ask, "Why didn't you support and help Yancy and Whitney (my sister) become who I called them to be?" As my earthly father, I've seen my dad (and my mom) give and sacrifice to help us answer God's call. As lucky as I am to call him dad, I know he's also a spiritual father to many. He's worked in the local church my whole life and then some. He doesn't take his role lightly. He has the biggest heart of anyone I know. He is also the most positive glass-half-full person I know. He has spent decades investing in younger leaders so that they can go on to do even greater things because they have learned from his mistakes and his example. His spiritual-father heart is the same. He wants to help you become who God created you to be.

In this book, you'll read words from my dad that, at times, will make you laugh, and at other times, they will challenge and inspire you. If you'll let the words written on these pages soak into your life, I know you'll see growth. As you read these nuggets of wisdom and tweetable phrases of leadership, I hope you'll dream new dreams and raise the bars that you've previously set. More than anything, I hope that you'll become all that God created you to be.

As a songwriter, I write songs that use words to tell a story. The marriage between lyrics and melody helps people feel something. It creates a memory that isn't easily forgotten. The songs I sing don't just tell a story but many times also help us learn. When we sing along, the songs we sing become a confession.

As a worship leader, I love the hiding place that we find in the presence of the Lord. Time after time, worship songs I've sung have helped remind me what I believe, especially when I need to remember the vast greatness of God. These songs help me speak what I know is true about God, even when my situations have made me feel the opposite. I've realized that the words I sing are a confession. And your confession matters. Words have power. What you say and speak matters.

Life is full of seasons. There are different phases of life that each of us is trying to navigate through. Some stages of life and leadership are much easier than others. But, whether life is rosy or gloomy, we have our words. We choose how to use them. We allow words to be spoken whether in our mind, the mirror, or reality. You can build situations, ministries, and people up; or you can tear them down. The difference is the words you speak.

My dad spoke words into my heart that grew and flourished into something beautiful, just as he will speak words into your life through the pages of this book. I hope they will grow and expand your heart. May new chapters unfold and new dreams be dreamed.

May old challenges be conquered and new ones climbed to tell an incredible story of God's faithfulness and provision in your life and ministry.

Today, I am a proud daughter. I get to call Jim Wideman my dad, and for that I am grateful. I am proud to be a second-generation children's minister. No matter what tomorrow holds, I know that God is the Giver of all good things. And I will forever believe in the power of our words.

Yancy

President and Founder

Yancy Ministries, Inc.

www.yancynotnancy.com

Introduction

It's amazing the power of just a few words. Proverbs 17:27-28 TLB says, "The man of few words and settled mind is wise; therefore, even a fool is thought to be wise when he is silent. It pays him to keep his mouth shut." We all look smarter when we follow this advice. Because of Twitter™ and social media, the world has become full of one-liners, quotes, and words of wisdom in just 144 characters.

When I jumped into the Twitterverse back in 2007, I began tweeting about how I think and what I have learned about leadership. Along the way, people started telling me that I needed to compile a book of all of my sayings and one-liners. In fact, I started this book about five years ago as a project for one of my Infuse groups, but every time I'd start working on it, I just couldn't get the right formula for the book. After a lot of help from my Infusers and tons of prayer, I got the vision for what this project needed to be. Not all these things came from me; I grew up hearing tons of one-liners and wise sayings from my mom. I've always told people that I'm a lot like Forest Gump—we're both from Alabama and our mothers were always telling us wise sayings to live by. Over the years, a lot of those who have listened to my teachings have referred to these words of wit as Jim-isms. A few years ago, several of my Infusers and coaches went through all of my books and teachings and helped me select and underline some of the greatest hits of the things I've said, tweeted, and written. That's what this book is—a collection of leadership tidbits and snippets from my life and writings. I've also added some of my favorite articles and thoughts I've gathered along the way. My prayer is that in just a few words, the thoughts and principles inside this book will get inside you and help change your thinking. Why is it so important that our thinking be changed? That's simple: our actions come from our thoughts. So if we want different actions and outcomes, it starts with changing the way we think.

I've found that the voice of wisdom and the voice of God are always the same. I've also learned along the way that a stronghold is just believing wrong thinking or wrong information. So if I want to tear down the strongholds in my life, I have to start by getting rid of the wrong thoughts or stinking thinking I've bought into.

Today can be a new day for your career, your family, and your thinking. My prayer for you is that the things you read in this book cause you to stop and think about them. Let them help change your thinking and thus change your actions and processes. A thought doesn't have to be huge or lengthy to be timely or to produce change. In Psalm 19:14 it says, "May these words of my mouth and this meditation of my heart be pleasing in your sight, Lord, my Rock and my Redeemer." That's my prayer for this project: that these words and tweets will line up with God's Word and produce encouragement, wisdom, and new thinking in your life, your ministry, and your family.

CH.

1

"

#JUSTSAYING

A LEADER IS AN EXAMPLE

"

1.
Things are
not as bad as
you think they
are and you're not
as wonderful
as you think you
are! It's always
somewhere
in between.

"

2. Don't make the same mistake twice; there are enough different ones you can make every time.

3. When everything is said and done, there's a lot more said than done.

4. God is never late, but He's seldom early.

5. Grow tough skin, but keep a tender heart in both ministry and business.

6. There's more than one way to skin a cat (i.e., don't get locked into only one way of doing things).

7. What's good for the goose is good for the gander (you must set the example for what you want others to do).

8. If you don't leave, you can't come back (i.e., go home: it will all be waiting for you when you return).

9

If you aim at nothing,
you'll hit it every time.
#planahead

"

10.
Experience is the best teacher, but it doesn't have to be your experiences that you learn from.

"

11.   Fifteen minutes early is on time.

12.   Common sense isn't always common.

13.   When God closes a door, He always opens a window.

14.   Your actions come from your thinking.

15.   When you live in a glass house, you learn to dress in the basement; sometimes you forget the house is glass, and it gets ugly.

16.   I didn't just need a savior when I found Jesus; I still need Him.

17.   It's never too late to change; we serve the God of a second chance.

18.   You can't be an effective coach if you are not willing to be a constant learner.

19.   Learning on a regular basis calls for intentional choices to humble yourself.

20.   Before you start next year's file, take time to celebrate the accomplishments of others now.

21. A big part of learning is humbling yourself enough to be taught.

22. I get more out of watching those I've trained do ministry than doing it myself. #legacy

23. You have to sneak up on your church or business to see it through the eyes of a first-time visitor or customer.

24. I know a lot of stuff, and most of it doesn't apply anymore (i.e., don't be satisfied with old accomplishments).

25. Growth, change, or leadership development is a process, not a pill.

26. If you find yourself hammering a square peg into a round hole, and it's slow going, don't blame the peg or the hammer. It's your fault.

27. Ministry, as well as business, is all about relationships.

28. Effectiveness in ministry starts and ends with loving people.

29. Who we are and how we live affects other people.

30. I think Christians should act like Christ. #justsaying

31. Worship is not about us; it's about Jesus.

32. You can learn something every day if you want to. The key is to want to.

33. If you can be thankful, you can be thank-empty. I choose to be thank-full.

34. Today is a gift! Enjoy it and the people God has placed around you.

35. Growing leadership isn't about just doing; it's about being someone worth following, and it develops from the inside out.

36. Sometimes people are more satisfied with old problems than new solutions.

37. Do not let your ministry replace your personal walk with Christ.

"

38.
You can lead in two ways: what's comfortable for you, or what's best for your team. The choice is up to you.

"

39.   I just want to be a pair of overalls the Holy Spirit can put on and use to get Jesus' work done.

40.   Effective leaders value people's feelings, but they also value moving ahead to get done what God wants as well.
It's both/and.

41.   Most leaders say they have a strategy, but they are not strategic in what they do.

42.   Sacred cows make the best burgers.

43.   Life is too short to not have fun.

44.   God is moved by faith, not by needs.

45.   Get a reputation for humility, for giving the glory to Jesus, and for having integrity.

46.   You are going to have to do things you've never done before if you want results you've never had before.

47

You can love the Lord
without loving the Word;
but if you love the Word, it will
show you how to love the Lord.

48.   Leaders don't focus on what they're lacking—they focus on where they are going and how to get there.

49.   Why would the Lord trust you with more sheep when you can't take care of the ones you have?

50.   I've dedicated my life to helping kids not turn out like their parents, including my own.

51.   There are people counting on you in the future to follow what God is asking you to do today.

52.   The modern church must be committed to reaching the modern family.

53.   Fear is faith in reverse.

54.   Choose to be flexible, or you'll break and have to be replaced.

55.   Most growing churches don't do anything that resembles the denomination or group they are a part of.

56.   The key to growing others is identifying which parts inside of you need to change.

57.   Every time I meet with another leader, I have questions ready that I want to ask so I can learn from them. How about you? What do you want to learn today?

58.   Just because you are called by God doesn't mean you aren't going to have stressful situations in your life and family.

59.   The brain is for thinking and dreaming, not for remembering.

"

A Leader Is
an Example

"

Have you ever been told, "Do as I say, not as I do"? When I was a teen, it made me mad. I still don't like it when leaders think there is a different set of rules for them than for the people they lead. In 1 Corinthians 11:1, Paul lets us know that leaders should be examples: "Follow my example, as I follow the example of Christ." The starting place for any leader is giving himself a check-up from the neck up and examining his own integrity.

Integrity is uprightness of character. It's honesty. It's lining up with God's Word. For people with integrity, their word is their bond. When they say they'll do something, they do it. Promises matter. And what they say they believe is reflected in their actions.

To lead in ministry, you don't have to be right all the time—which is a relief for me because I flunked the perfection test a long time ago. But you do need to give up the desire to have people think you're always right.

Admit it: you like having people think you're right. It's just human, especially when you're a leader. You think it builds confidence in the troops when they see you make decisions and stick to your guns.

Except we aren't always right. We're wrong a lot. And people don't admire leaders who are too proud or scared to admit they don't know it all.

When you're willing to let others know you—the real you—then you'll have integrity. But if your leadership depends on people not knowing what you believe or what you do when you're flipping through the cable channels or surfing the net, then you'll never be an effective leader. You've got to get your own house in order before trying to lead others.

Are you willing to be a leader who doesn't just talk about integrity but lives it? This kind of leader desires to become an example worthy of being imitated. What and who we are shapes what we do. Christ Jesus did not tell His disciples to believe in Him but to follow Him (Mark 2:14). The key to being His sheep is following Him. John 10:27 tells us, "My sheep listen to my voice; I know them, and they follow me." John 12:26 also says, "Whoever serves me must follow me."

You may have heard me teach about the five duties of a shepherd from 1 Peter 5:2-4:

Be shepherds of God's flock that is under your care, serving as overseers—not because you must, but because you are willing, as God wants you to be; not greedy for money, but eager to serve; not lording it over those entrusted to you, but being examples to the flock. And when the Chief Shepherd appears, you will receive the crown of glory that will never fade away.

In these verses, we see five main duties or descriptions of a shepherd:

1. Feeder
2. Caregiver
3. Overseer
4. Willing and Eager Servant
5. Example

What qualifies you to do the top four and truly be a leader is your willingness and desire to be an example. Being an example is more important than talent.

First Timothy 4:12 says, "Don't let anyone look down on you because you are young, but set an example for the believers in speech, in life, in love, in faith and in purity." Titus 2:6-8 says, "Encourage the young men to be self-controlled. In everything set them an example by doing what is good. In your teaching show integrity, seriousness and soundness of speech that cannot be condemned, so those who oppose you may be ashamed because they have nothing bad to say about us." Children need role models, and so do the adults we lead and the staff we direct. If leaders desire to be examples, we should be examples of . . .

First, examples of Christ Jesus and followers of Him. Salvation is the starting place, not the end. The great commission isn't to go make decisions but disciples. It's simple; I must be a disciple to make disciples.

A follower is more than a believer; a follower is also a doer of the Word. John 14:15 is very plain. Jesus says, "If you love me, you will obey what I command."

Whatever we have listed as "requirements to serve" on our worker applications should be modeled in our own lives. I desire that my life and choices show I have been born again, and that I'm in agreement with my church's Statement of Faith (agreement means practice). It's always the correct choice to practice what we preach, to live the Bible twenty-four seven. To me, holiness is not just saying no to wrong things, it's saying yes to the right

Choose to
be flexible,
or you'll
break and
have to
be replaced.

things. It's always the right thing to model being a giver. Make it a practice to run from the appearance of evil just like the real thing.

If you've heard any of my leadership lessons or read any of my books, you know I believe your family is your greatest sermon. Leaders must have their home lives in order. I love Proverbs 28:2; it says, "When a country is rebellious, it has many rulers, but a man of understanding and knowledge maintains order." This begins with evaluating daily if Christ is truly King of our hearts and our choices. I ask myself on a regular basis, "Has there ever been a time in my life where I have been more in love with Jesus than I am right now?" If I can ever say yes, I fix it.

Secondly, we should be examples of flowing with authority or being submitted to the leadership above us. Lots of leaders claim to be loyal to their pastors and leadership, but the proof of this attitude is reflected in their actions.

You're really not loyal to your leader if you treat his or her representatives differently than you treat the leader. Being teachable is also a form of submission to authority; fighting change is not standing with authority. It's always right to say no to sowing seeds of discord. Sharing a non-biblical opinion with others can be a form of this. Gossip is never a good thing.

Going where you're needed is an example of one who is under authority. Jesus said if you have seen Him, you have seen the Father. Can that be said of us? If people see us, do they also see those we represent and serve?

Third, we should be examples of commitment and faithfulness. It takes time to establish relationships. Every time I commit more and practice being faithful to establish deeper relationships, I grow as a leader. Helping others find their fit within your team will help them make and model commitment. Kids, as well as adults, need an example of consistency. Always come when you are needed. (It's sad that you can stick out in ministry just by showing up on time. My mom always taught me that early is on time.) Dependable people can be leaned on, so the ultimate question is can you be leaned on no matter what?

We should show our commitment not only to our ministry but also to our senior pastor. Go to church. Ministry is like a checkbook: you have to make deposits before you can write checks. Model faithfulness to take in as well as to give out. Desire to be an example for others.

Be an example to your workers of what you want them to do. Also be an example to parents of what you want them to do. Model to the kids what you want them to be, and give them the Word on it. It's up to each leader to make his or her **want to** the same as **expected to.**

Lastly, be an example of excellence in ministry. Always be prepared by studying to show yourself approved. Learn and grow constantly. You have to model this to others if you want them to do the same. It's up to you, leader, to give others an example to follow. No matter what your title, you are not a true leader if you're not an example. Remember, a leader must set the pace. A leader must be honest. A leader must be loyal. A leader leaves no one behind without a helper.

Being the example you need to be qualifies you to feed and care for the flock, so oversee and be willing and able to serve. Your integrity fuels your ability to be the example you need to be to others and to be the leader you desire to be.

You can learn something everyday if you want to! The key is to want to!

CH.

2

"

#KIDS #FAMILY AND #PARENTING

DEVELOPING A BIBLICAL WORLD VIEW IN YOUR CHILDREN

66

60.
Any man can be a father, but a daddy has a relationship with his kids.

99

61. God gave parents the responsibility to train their kids in spiritual things and bring them up in the ways of the Lord, not the church.

62. Parents should train their children from an early age to go to God for direction. They learn this best by seeing you model it.

63. Children are looking for someone who will stand up and say, "Follow me as I follow God"; instead of, "Do as I say not as I do."

64. The time I spent with my daughters while they were young was an investment of love that is now paying rich dividends in my old age.

65. Giving is a natural response from a loving father to his children.

66. One of the things I've learned from my heavenly Father is to reward my kids for doing good; always be on the lookout for opportunities to bless them.

67

You need to realize that
you have to demonstrate
as well as communicate
your love to your family every day,
not just when it's convenient
or when you feel like it.

"

68.
Whatever you did to win your spouse's affection is the same thing you must do to keep it.

"

69. Kids who don't have a close relationship with a loving father will seek the attention of other men who will give it. I don't want someone else taking my place.

70. Good or bad, the way you treat your spouse is what your children will grow up to believe is normal.

71. Children can be demanding and try to move up on the priority list, but it's important to remember that your spouse comes before you kids.

72. As a children's pastor, I work hard to make church a fun place for kids. If I do this for the children at church, why can't I do this for the kids at my house?

73. You must always explain to your children why their actions were not acceptable; show them what the Word of God says about their choices and their actions.

74. Your kids need you more than the stuff you work long hours to provide for them. They need you, so make time for them now.

75. I don't believe there is such a thing as a problem child. I've only met children with problems.

76. Good parents are consistent in their discipline; anything else just causes kids to be confused about what the rules are.

77. After your have disciplined your children, don't forget to pray with them; and most of all, hug them and let them know that you love them.

78. Never discipline out of anger. It will keep you from doing something you'll have to apologize for later.

79. Children rule in a divided home; God rules in a united one.

80. Recognize that God created your children differently; allow them to be different.

81. A common mistake parents make is that they compare their children to each other when they know God made them unique.

82. Parents who step into their children's worlds and find out what interests them sow seeds for their children to show an interest in their worlds too.

83. Talk to your children about everything early, and they'll talk to you about everything when they are older.

84. One of the best ways to stay close to older kids is to be kind to their friends.

85. Don't open the door for rebellion in your children's lives by rebelling against authority yourself.

86. When your kids know that you periodically check up on them, they're more likely to always be where they tell you they are going.

87. You must model to your children that failures do not keep them from success. It's how they choose to deal with those failures that determine if they'll be successful or not.

"

88.
Training on the job or in the home involves more show than tell.

"

89. The number-one mistake in teaching the Bible to children is to fill them with facts instead of the principles of each story and teaching.

90. Look for every opportunity to build memories with your immediate family.

91. I learned years ago that kids don't spell love L-O-V-E. They spell it T-I-M-E and M-O-N-E-Y. It's important that they receive both from you.

92. As a parent, show your children by example how to pray and stand on the Word to overcome life's hard situations.

93. Let your family be your greatest achievement in life. (They've been my greatest sermon yet).

94

The best thing you can do
for your kids is to love your spouse
the way you want their spouses
to love them.

" Developing a Biblical Worldview in Your Children "

I had no idea that saying yes to the command, "Get your guitar and your Bible, and go back to children's church" from my pastor in 1977 would change my life forever. Not only has it changed me as a person and as a Christ-follower, it's changed me as a husband, a father, an employee, and a minister. It has changed the lens I view everything through. It began a journey that at sixty years young and counting I'm still on—to know God and love His Word and to help sons and daughters do the same.

I've told this story for years, but it bears repeating. For three years, I had been working with teenagers serving in churches and playing in a Christian rock-and-roll band when my pastor came looking for me and told me to go cover children's church. The teacher had called in last minute and informed my pastor that she was not coming back. I wanted to help my pastor, so

NOTES:

I did what he said. I grabbed my guitar and Bible, and I went back to the old fellowship hall to find seven kids in the class. How hard could this be? I thought.

The answer came just moments into the hour and a half that turned into what seemed like a month. It was the hardest thing I had ever done on short notice. I was not pre-pared, and the kids could smell the fresh blood like a school of sharks. They ate me up! I went to find my pastor as soon as the last child had been picked up. I wanted to know how long I was going to have to do this. I'll never forget Brother Wilson's reply, "You'll need to do it until God raises up someone with a vision."

Immediately I began to pray, "Lord, give someone a vision for children's ministry! Open their eyes, Lord, and let them see the importance of reaching and teaching kids from Your viewpoint." After praying that prayer and working with the children over the next several weeks, I soon realized I was that someone that Jesus had given the vision to.

How did I come to this realization? I had begun to see children's ministry from a differ-ent viewpoint, a biblical viewpoint. For the first time ever as a young Christ-follower, I began to see that children and the importance of ministering to them is in the Bible. I've tried to do other things in ministry, but that vision, that viewpoint, would not leave me. I believe what's missing from so many ministries and families is an understanding of life from a biblical worldview.

Just like the church needs a biblical vision for reaching children, so parents need a vision for reaching their children. God designed the family to put His Word into future gener-ations. Have you ever asked God what He wants for your family? You can ask Him for His vision for your family, or you can continue walking blindly forward. But remember, if you aim at nothing, you'll hit it every time.

So since God gives you the desires of your heart, what are your desires and goals for your children? For me, I wanted our family to be close. I wanted them to love the Lord with all their hearts and to love the Word. In fact, I wanted them to love the Bible so much that they based every life choice on it. What about you? What's on your list? Take a break from reading, and start a list right now. Then ask God if your list is His list.

The Bible is the benchmark of how we should view the world and live. My goal for my children, as well as every child I have the opportunity to teach and pastor, is for them to grow up to become doers of the Word. I realized early in my ministry that children couldn't live what they couldn't remember, and they couldn't remember what they didn't understand. It changed the way I taught, the methods I used, and how visual and simply I needed to communicate; but most of all, I realized they needed a model or example. Show is needed along with the tell. That is what Deuteronomy 6 is all about—parents making every available minute count that they have with their children, modeling a love for the Lord and His Word. Parents must be as intentional and visual as pastors or teachers. Imagine if all of us, the church and the family, worked together for one purpose.

Over these past forty-plus years of working with children, I've seen thousands of kids come up through my ministry. I am so blessed to have scores of Timothys (young people that I have had an influence on who enter the ministry) in full-time ministry who were once in my children's church. I have gotten a real kick out of catching up with kids on Facebook™ who have been a part of previous children's ministries I have had the privilege of leading. But the sad spot within my heart is when I think about the kids who are not living for Christ and who are not walking out the goal to become a doer of the Word. The problem is not just in the church; it's also in the home. So many kids who were not only raised in the church but were also raised in Christian homes by Christian parents, listening to Christian music, watching Christian videos, reading Christian books, hanging around with Christian friends who did the same things are not following Christ today. What happened? I believe that the problem lies within the church and the family having two different views of life rather than one Bible-based worldview.

As a parent, show your children by example how to pray and stand on the Word to overcome life's hard situations.

The Bible tells us we are in the world, but we are not of the world. The Bible also tells us to come out of the world and be separate, yet we are told to be salt and light to the world. Over the years, I have studied families and the different ways they parent. I've also studied churches and the different ways they do church. To me, the families and the churches who have the greatest success are the ones who have teamed together to join forces to develop in each individual a biblical view of how to live 24/7. I have had the honor of raising two wonderful daughters. They are both successful, not only in business but also in their spiritual walks. (One of them even contributed to this book—talk about a blessing.) My girls are as different as night and day; if I had not been in the delivery room with both of them, I would not believe they are kin. I have had to discipline them differently; I have to communicate and instruct them differently. But when it comes down to making choices about how to live, it was the same for them as it was for their mother and me—what does the Bible say?

There are lots of voices that speak into our lives that challenge a biblical worldview. As a parent and as a pastor, I cannot block out every voice that speaks to my family and to my congregation, nor should I. But I have spent my life pointing out that God's Word contains Truth, and the Truth of the Word is what will set us free. God's Word is the filter we should view the world through. Years ago I learned that a stronghold is simply believing wrong information. When we take captive every thought and make it obedient to the Word of God, it produces right thinking, which creates right actions. Our actions come from our thinking; that's why we have to be intentional about the voices we listen to and the actions we do, regardless of our age. When my children were small, we limited the voices and the "traditions we planted in our children." Just because a movie or TV show was animated or geared for children didn't mean we allowed our children to feed on it. We have never lied to our children. We never told them there was a tooth fairy; Daddy bought their teeth. We never told them their Christmas presents came from the North Pole or were made by elves. We told them the stories as stories, not as truth. The truth was their presents came from Mom and Dad with love bought with money Father God provided us because He loves His kids and wants us to love ours.

One of the reasons my children believed me about Jesus is because we never lied to them. When I told them about the hurt and pain from living contrary to God's Word, they believed me. They didn't need to experience the pain themselves; they learned from my mistakes and believed me because I've always told them the truth. I learned when I first started working with kids to always keep your promises to them. I never made a promise in children's church that I couldn't keep. If I did that at church, I needed to do that at home. I never promised I would be at everything. I told my girls I would try, and I was honest if there were a possibility that I could not be there. I'm not saying I've never disappointed my children. I have many times, but I've told them the truth about life and tried to model what I was asking them to do and believe.

So with these things in mind, here's my top-ten list as a children's pastor and a dad on how to instill in your kids a biblical worldview:

1. *Always be open and honest with your children about every subject.* One thing I see in the ministry of Jesus is that He was never too busy for questions. Encourage your kids to ask questions. Listen to what they are asking, and give them a why as well as a what. If you freak out, then they'll stop asking. Help them understand that there is a difference between a question, a doubt, and unbelief. Never be too busy for questions—a big part of that is spending time with your kids. The more time you spend with them and the less you freak out, the more questions they'll ask at home and at church.

2. *Model to children what you want them to do when they grow up, and place other models around them.* Never forget: when it comes to Bible living, when you point at others, there are three fingers pointing back at you. There can't be one set of rules for you and another for them. Follow Paul's words as he says, "Come follow me as I follow Christ" (1 Cor.

You can learn something everyday if you want to! The key is to want to!

NOTES:

11:1.) At the heart of Deuteronomy 6 is the fact that the parents must set the example: "These commandments that I give you today are to be on your hearts" (Deut. 6:6).

3. *Teach principles, not facts.* The number-one mistake in teaching the Bible to children is to fill them with facts instead of instilling in them the principles of each story and teaching. Facts go in our heads, while principles go in our hearts and help us to walk out the truths within. Kids need the principles of the Word to apply it to their everyday lives. Do your children at home and at church know the principles within the stories or just the stories?

4. *Let children know wisdom is better than money or fame.* One of the greatest lessons I ever learned is that the voice of wisdom and the voice of God is always the same thing. That's why I need to know God's Word because it also contains His wisdom. The world tells kids life is about fame and fortune. I know more parents who are more concerned with their child's ability to produce wealth than to instill the pursuit of wisdom and truth above all. The Bible says that wisdom is better than riches or gold. If someone is wise, that wisdom will bring blessing, honor, and a good name. Knowledge is the beginning of wisdom, and God's wisdom brings blessings. Have you instilled this principle in your child?

5. *Just because it's on TV or in a movie doesn't make it right or true.* I'm not sure when the TV changed roles with parents, but in many households it has. Because of the craziness of our schedules, we never really watched any TV programs when they came on; we recorded them and watched them later. It turned out to be a tremendous blessing because we were able to fast forward through some stuff and pause and talk about other stuff. When I was a child, Lucy and Ricky couldn't even sleep in the same bed. Today our kids are bombarded with messages contrary to the Bible. Whether it's a TV program or the news, you need to tell your children the truth. It's seems like all the media wants to talk about is bad news. I know there are some things that need to be reported, but I want to point out the promises of God that work in every type of econ-

omy. We still serve a God who is more than enough. He is our supply and our provider. Feel free to correct the wrong voices, and remind kids what the Bible says. Here's a wonderful project for both church and home: have your child choose a topic or a viewpoint to research. Using television shows, movies, magazines, and newspapers, have them write down what the media says about that topic, and then have them research what the Bible says. Let them see for themselves how the two points of view are different.

6. *The Bible is the infallible Word of God and has the answers for everything in life.* Whatever the answer you are looking for, it's in God's Word. How should I treat others? Whom should I forgive? Whom should I be a friend with? How should I treat my parents, my family, or my employer? Whom should I vote for? What should our nation's views on Israel be? It's all in the Book! It's not just for Sundays and Wednesdays; it's for Mondays, Tuesdays, Thursdays, Fridays, and Saturdays too. This is the guidebook on living and the filter that every voice should be measured against. God's Word is not outdated. It's relevant for today. One of the things you can do with your children both at home and church is to gather the questions kids need to answer, and then give them the answers from God's Word.

7. *Jesus is the only way to the Father, and He lived a sinless life by following the words of the Scripture.* Every time Jesus faced the devil or demonic opposition, He spoke the Word. Our tongue has the power of life and death. When we speak the Word, we speak words of life. As parents and pastors, we need to help kids watch their words and be intentional about saying what the Word says. This is also how we build our faith. Faith comes by hearing. When we say God's Word, it pumps us up and builds our faith like reps with dumbbells and barbells. We should all be asking and teaching kids to ask, "What would Jesus do?" Then we should do it. What confessions should you lead your children in to get God's Word in their hearts? One scripture I have taught my children, as well as one I say often, is "I am the Lord's sheep; He is my shepherd. I know His voice. The voice of a stranger I won't hear."

These commandments that I give you today are to be on your hearts.

DEUT. 6:6

8. *Point out wrong thinking anywhere you experience it, and don't let it lay roots.* The children in our churches as well as the children in our homes need to see that what the Word says and what the world says can be different. When we are faced with a choice, we choose the Word. Take advantage of teachable moments anywhere anytime. Kids don't need devotions; they need to be taught to live a devoted life based on the Word. Dare to confront and challenge wrong thinking in the media. As you do life, take every opportunity you are given to make God's Word real to your kids. I not only jump into my own girls' lives, I jump into the kids' lives that I teach and lead at church. To me, if you love any group of kids, you'll look for opportunities to swap wrong thinking for truth and love them enough to confront them in love. What do the children around you need to hear?

9. *Quote the Bible to your kids, and let them see you feed on the Word constantly.* What's good for the goose is good for the gander. You should model to children and families a life built on the Word. If your kids don't see you doing these things, they won't do them either. If we are what we eat physically, we are also what we eat spiritually. The more I pray, read, and meditate on the Word, it helps the kids around me do the same. When kids ask for your advice, give them the Word. They need the Word more than anything else you can give them. Recently at a conference, I overheard some people talking about the workshops I had taught, and they were telling some people to go to my workshops because I actually use the Bible. Now if I can stick out at a conference by using the Bible, you can also stick out as a parent for giving your children the Word.

10. *Teach the importance of attending and being active in church.* One of my favorite scriptures is Luke 4:16. It tells us that Jesus went to the synagogue on the Sabbath day, as was His custom. Jesus modeled for us the habit of attending church. It was never up for discussion whether my daughters would attend church or not. If they wanted to take a dance class on a church night, they didn't take the class. They went to church. But not only did they attend, they served. They were active in ministries for their age group, and they also gave back to others. I was not the only person in our family involved in ministry; we were a ministering family. Now that they are adults, they are still doing what they were trained as children to do. Yancy is in full-time ministry, but she still gives back to her home church. Whitney doesn't just attend a small group; she's the small-group leader. Parents, if you make them eat green beans because "they are good for you," why not have them in church? It is also good for them. Don't just tell them to do it: set the example of attending, serving, learning, and growing.

Do the children at your church and the children at your house have a love for the Bible—a love that moves them from studying the Bible to living the Bible? It's not just the responsibility of the pastor; it's both the home and the church doing these things together.

Come follow me as I follow Christ.

1 COR. 11:1

CH.

#LEADERSHIP LESSONS

A GROWING LEADER IS A LEARNER

"

95.
All churches and businesses have problems. Find a set of problems you want to spend the rest of your life fixing, and then fix them.

"

96. I've dreamed all of my life of getting to face the problems and challenges I face It's an honor.

97. Vision is just seeing how God wants things to end up.

98. As a role-model leader, Jesus was never too busy for questions; we can't be too busy either.

99. Positional leadership is the lowest form of leadership. You must give people a reason to esteem you.

100. People follow people with a plan.

101. I've got some good news and some bad news— the good news is I will never ask you to do anything that I'm not willing to do. The bad news is that I'm willing to do just about anything.

102. Anytime you don't know where you are, you're lost.

103

If God leads us in steps,
why don't we think in steps?

> **66**
>
> # 104.
> A leader can walk in a room and see more than just four walls: he sees opportunities and room for improvement.
>
> **99**

105. God shows a vision to you because you're the one He wants and has called to pull it off.

106. Some people like to have their team operate like the Department of Transportation—one guy with a shovel and three guys watching. Not me. I give everyone a shovel, put one in charge, and tell them to get after it; then it gets done in a quarter of the time.

107. A leader points the way and sets the pace.

108. A leader must see things first before they can come to pass.

109. You can't lead if you don't know where you're going.

110. Effective leaders don't have a big vision: a big vision has them.

111. There are a lot of places the buck can stop before it gets to the leader if the leader delegates authority along with responsibility.

112. If you find yourself in the middle of a war at work, it doesn't matter who started it, but it does matter who ends it.

113. Good leaders develop their skills so they can be problem solvers, encouragers, cheerleaders, and coaches. The hard part is doing them all at one time.

114. It's not enough for the leader to have and know the vision; they must effectively communicate that vision to the people around them.

115. Ministry is like a checkbook. If you don't make deposits, you can't write checks.

116. There are two words that I don't pay attention to anymore—big and busy. Their definitions change all the time.

117. Every Monday I used to think about quitting, but my vision wouldn't let me. That's why you need a vision!

118. God doesn't expect you to do what you can't do, but He does expect you to do what you can do.

119. There are tons of folks better looking with more talents and abilities than you; but if you're willing, nobody has to outwork you.

120. All you need to move ahead is to take the next step.

121. If you think your next step is really a leap or a jump, then it's not from God.

122. Understanding your organization's past will help you understand your organization's definitions.

123. Too much too quick is a real trick of the enemy.

124. Counting the cost doesn't happen just once.

125. If you're not making mistakes, you're not trying anything new.

126. In order to be a good leader, you must first be a good follower.

"

127.
Successful leaders make mistakes, and then they learn from those mistakes and keep going.

"

128.   Having information doesn't make you a leader, but it's essential to your success to be well-informed.

129.   You can tell a lot about a leader by the people he keeps around him.

130.   You can't fix what you don't evaluate needs fixing.

131.   Take what you do seriously, but don't take yourself too seriously.

132.   Watch out for too many babies in the crib (i.e., don't start a bunch of new stuff all at once). There's a reason single births are easier to manage than multiple births.

133.   Answer your phone! It will immediately improve how others view your leadership.

134.   Ministry looks a whole lot like work.

135.   If the size of your ministry or business doubled, which tasks are you doing now that you would be forced to not do anymore? Go ahead and train someone to do those now.

—

136

True leaders grow from
the inside out—their leadership
begins with their character because
we are all made in the image of God.

—

137. It is important to see your ministry as half full, not half empty. Perspective makes all the difference in the world.

138. Three keys to growth:
- Expand your structure.
- Keep doing only the things that brought you success.
- Don't be afraid to try new stuff.

139. It's great to respect tradition, but don't confuse it with Scripture or the voice of God.

140. Children's ministers work with one group of children, but their everyday duties involve three groups of adults: parents, adult workers, and other staff.

141. Without leadership, children's and youth ministers are just educators and entertainers.

142. High tech calls for high touch. People are the difference makers within any organization.

143. Effective leaders don't walk away from problems or challenges—they squarely face them. They don't float through life or walk past broken situations—they get involved.

144. Innovators and problem solvers will always have a job and be in high demand.

145. Choose to be a part of the solution, not the problem.

146. It is your job to make sure your vision clearly aligns with your leader's vision.

147. A leader is a learner.

148. Burnout happens when you stay overwhelmed for long periods of time.

149. Those who give up and move on seldom find greener grass in other places.

150. Every church staff member should give the senior pastor what that leader wants. We need to all be working toward the same goal—the vision of the house.

151.   I have no problems that are more important than my leader's problems.

152.   Has there ever been a time in your life that you are more in love with Jesus than you are right now? If so, you're the only one that can do something about it.

153.   The things we do for one person mean more to them than what we do for thousands.

154.   The time you invest in people development is never wasted.

155.   Just because something worked in the past doesn't mean it's the best way to do things now.

156.   I like my steaks rare, but I want my works to be well done.

"

157.

Ask yourself on a regular basis, "What in my life has become more about me and less about Jesus?"

"

> **"**
>
> # A Growing Leader is a Leader
>
> **"**

After years of watching children's ministry leaders fail to see their dreams come true, I noticed a common problem. Most workers and leaders in the local church just don't see the need to continually learn. To me learning is not something that's optional; it is a must. Being a learner must be a part of your everyday lifestyle if you are serious about growing. When I was in college, I learned the smartest and most intelligent response to any question or situation is "I don't know." There's nothing wrong with not knowing it all. I don't understand why people think it's wrong to say I don't know. The key is to let I don't know move you to I'll find out. There is nothing wrong with admitting you don't know how to do something either.

When I moved to Tulsa in 1990, my new church was basically the same size as the previous three churches I had worked at. But as we grew during the seventeen years I was there, every Sunday I went to church, that was the largest church I had ever been a part of. I didn't know how to do what I was being asked to do every weekend, which forced me to explore and learn. The intensity of how you pursue exploring and learning is the true sign that sets you apart as a leader. Study makes work approved. One of my favorite scriptures is 2 Timothy 2:15 KJV: "Study to show thyself approved unto God, a workman that needeth not to be ashamed, rightly dividing the word of truth." Approved work that is a direct result of study causes the workman to have no reason to be ashamed. We all know hard work pays off, but smart work is also important. Smart work comes from study and learning. When smart work and hard work are combined, great things happen. Smart work plus hard work always equals success. If you are reading this book, I know you want to bear fruit and be successful for the Lord, but your actions measure the intensity and passion of that quest. In evaluating my own journey, I'd like to give you twelve learning habits you should develop to stay fresh and current as a leader:

1. Develop a love for reading. I'm always on the lookout for a good book. I look for recommendations from people I look up to. I visit local bookstores and cruise the shelves of the business and leadership sections. I like to discuss what I'm reading with people who are also reading the same book. On Facebook™ I've listed some books I've read as well as those I want to read. I'm also a believer in re-reading a book and making sure I've put to use what I've already learned before I move on to a new book.

Also, it helps me to set a deadline to complete a book by. To meet that timeline, I try to keep a book with me at all times. I also buy one or two other books, so I'll have something ready to read when I finish my current book. They also help motivate me to finish the book I'm currently reading as I anticipate reading the new ones. I also enjoy blogging. There are some great blogs out there. I like to see who has linked to my blog, and I follow the link and see who else they read and check those authors out as well. Through this process, I have discovered some great learners to learn with.

2. *Listen to teaching.* We live in a wonderful time. There are so many teachings available to us such as MP3s, podcasts, and CDs. A great habit to form for learning is to regularly feed on information. I love my iPhone because I can keep teachings with me at all times. (For over twenty years now, I have been producing audio leadership teachings for children's ministers through my children's ministers leadership club. I make these available free of charge for leaders under 30, and for a low annual membership to those over 30. For more information go to http://www.jimwideman.com/the-club.html, or go to KidminCoach.com. Another benefit of listening to teaching is that I find myself re-listening to teachings more than I do re-reading books, which helps me process and learn the information faster.

3. *Ask questions.* This is my favorite way to learn. Jesus was the master of teaching and encouraging learning by questions. A growing faith is a questioning faith. I think fear of asking something dumb keeps us from taking advantage of this priceless method of learning. I believe with all my heart there is no such thing as a dumb question; there are dumb answers but no dumb questions if they are asked out of a sincere quest to learn. Any time you are with another leader that you value, take advantage of the opportunity to learn from him or her. Prepare questions ahead of time, and put them in order of importance. That way if you only have time for one or two questions, you get what you need. I get excited when someone pulls out a list of questions they want to ask me, but I have to admit it is not the norm. Most people don't view question-and-answer times as seriously as I do. It disappoints me when I conduct a Q & A session, and no one has a list of questions prepared.

Additionally, you can make a phone appointment with people you want to learn from, so you can pick their brains on subjects you need to learn about. Tell them what the subject or purpose of the call is when you set it up, and always email or fax your questions ahead of time. When you email a question, only email one question at a time. Never email more than one question per week.

Study to show thyself approved unto God, a workman that needeth not to be ashamed, rightly dividing the word of truth.

2 TIM 2:15

4. *Develop a relationship with people you esteem.* Years ago when I started in ministry, finding other children's pastors was not an easy task. There weren't many of us out there, so when I heard of another, I gave him a call. If I read an article that intrigued me, I contacted the author. I still email and call children's pastors and introduce myself and try to develop a relationship with those I want to know. When I see a hunger in other children's pastors, it gets my attention and causes me to draw close to them. But watch out for relationships that don't sharpen you. I am so thankful for the friendships I have both new and old that God uses to keep me thinking and growing.

5. *Use your lunches and dinners wisely.* A lunch meeting is a great time to put into others. I love to brainstorm over a meal with people I enjoy. I use the drive time to set the tone or agenda and the drive back to recap and make sure people understand the assignments or plan of action. A dinner meeting is a great way to connect with new people I want to get to know and learn from. Remember, the worst they can say is no. It's not about the food; it's about learning and brain-picking. I've even eaten before I go so I can take advantage of this time for me to learn.

6. *Visit other churches.* I love to tour churches wherever I go, and when I do, I take lots of pictures. There are several churches I've visited more than once, and every time I've gone, I've picked up new ideas. I love to visit churches with multiple locations to see what changes they made when they had a chance to redo their children's space. It's very eye opening to see what others do firsthand. Get outside your church, and take a road trip to visit churches with creative and unique children's ministries so you can see what you can learn.

7. *Go to conferences.* I love to attend conferences for many more reasons than just the sessions. I love to hear and see what has worked for others. I like to take others along with me to expose them to bigger thinking. A picture is worth a thousand words. When others go to conferences that I did not attend, I try to identify what they saw and learned so I can learn through them.

8. *Network—surround yourself with peers you respect.* Identify the ministry models available, and find out what they are presently thinking. Just because you heard them once doesn't mean you know what they are thinking and saying today. I want to know what any other person who has my position is doing and why. Sometimes knowing what not to do is just as important as knowing what to do. Always be on the lookout to find others who will discuss with you what they are learning. Seek to understand thinking different than your own. Be a fly on the wall, and listen to others as they discuss and network. A few years ago, I had the opportunity to have dinner with Sue Miller and Craig Jutilia. It was a wonderful time of learning and growing. As we were discussing our ministries, I was so proud of all the other children's pastors attending that event who pulled up a chair and just listened and learned as well.

9. *Study successful people.* I'm a huge fan of the TV series The Apprentice. I love to watch others lead so I can learn from them. I also enjoy reading the life stories about successful business people. Those kinds of books are my favorite. I also love to brainstorm or chat with others who also are fans.

10. *Get a leadership coach or hire a consultant to hold you accountable and to make you learn.* A view from another perspective can give you a huge advantage. If you are interested in coaching, be sure and check out Infuse at www.jimwideman.com/infuse.

How can I make all these things a part of my lifestyle? The best way I know is to get out your calendar, and plan. Set appointments and then do them. We all keep our appointments once we make them. Develop good learning habits, and repeat the same action until it becomes reflexive or second nature. Here are some of the places and situations where I like to read and listen: the treadmill and other exercise equipment; right before bedtime; I try to keep a book or two in the restroom at home and at work; planes; drive time; while I wait when I get a haircut or I am at the doctor. I even make appointments with myself to study and grow on a regular basis. Remember, study and learning doesn't have to be all at once; do it a little at a time.

Develop good learning habits, and repeat the same action until it becomes reflexive or second nature.

Expect those around you to learn. I ask my staff to include on their weekly reports: "What have you done for leadership development this past week?" You can't expect what you don't model, so why not make an intentional decision to set the pace and become an example of one who is always learning. It's up to you to stay fresh and current in your leadership skills and in your thinking. A growing leader is a learner.

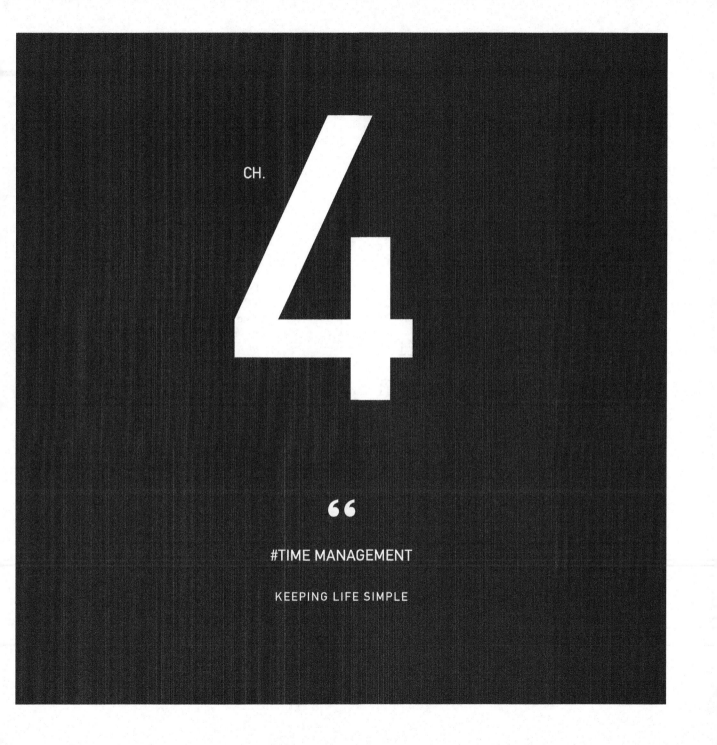

CH.

4

"

#TIME MANAGEMENT

KEEPING LIFE SIMPLE

"

158.
A lot of people think that people are either born organized or born without the ability to organize. Listen, we all came into this world the same way—naked.

"

159.   There is a difference between being busy and being effective.

160.   Busy is a relative term. It changes as your abilities increase.

161.   A lot of times, what people think is "too busy" is just "busy"; it's an indicator that your time management skills need some work.

162.   You make time for the things you want to make time for. The key is to want to do the right stuff—what God wants you doing.

163.   Calendars are like lawn mowers: whatever size yard God has made you a master over, you need the right size mower (calendar) to be able to handle it. You may need a tractor and livestock too.

164.   Your brain is not for remembering. That's your calendar's job. Your brain is for thinking and for dreaming.

165.   It's hard to manage time if you don't know what time it is. You need a watch.

—

166

One of the biggest time wasters
in the world are meetings—we
even have meetings to see
what meetings we need to have!

—

"

167.
Where and what we plan to spend our time doing should always be based on our priorities; this helps you make right decisions.

"

168. Appointments are the best way to schedule what you need to do. I keep my appointments even if I don't feel like doing them. I don't feel like going to the doctor when I'm sick, but I still make the appointment and keep it.

169. Evaluation is what separates time managers from calendar keepers, even really good calendar keepers.

170. When you delegate, you have access to the time of others, which opens your time up for more important tasks.

171. What are you doing that someone else can do? Use the time of others, and always look for opportunities to build a team.

172. It's not about how many hours you spend working each week; it's about what you accomplish that counts. Don't even worry about the hours. Just work. And when you're done, go play.

173. The best choices you can make as a leader is to evaluate your schedule on a daily basis and look for ways to improve it one day at a time.

174. There are really only two ways to get more time or to be able to get the most out of the time we already have: the first way is to organize and prioritize in order to eliminate time wasters; the second is to use the time of others.

175. Managing your time is a lot like managing your money. You must record how you're spending your time, and look at the things that you're doing that are wasteful.

176. When I use other people's time, it feels as if my time has multiplied because so much more is getting done, but I don't feel the burden of working those extra hours.

177. Don't get into the rut of filling your schedule with good choices when you can be focusing your time on God choices.

178. Being busy is not bad. It's being busy and not accomplishing what you need to that's bad.

179. Just like you can learn leadership principles, you can learn to be a better time manager.

180. The key is not just to manage what you're doing now but also to organize your time in such a way that you can manage increase.

181. Multitasking is working with multiple assigned pieces of work that all need to be finished within a similar timeframe.

182. It's imperative that you maintain control over your schedule. Don't let your schedule control you. Treat your time like it truly belongs to you.

183. What are you putting into others so that you can use their extra time?

184. Five secrets to practice daily to get more done:
    • Use the right tools.
    • Plan the events that you need to do, and plan the steps for those events.
    • Break it down into to-dos.
    • Evaluate daily.
    • Delegate to others.

"

185.
Never do business in the hallway; it's a good way to wet your pants.

"

186. Meeting rules:
- Select an end time, and then end on time!
- Use a timer to know when to quit.
- Place each item you have to share in order of importance.
- Stay on task.
- Stand up to talk when you want to make a point.
- Get feedback to find out if your meeting was helpful.

187. Here's the truth: people who manage their time well work less hours, not more.

188. Don't mistake activity for making progress.

189. Time management is the greatest tool in a leader's toolbox.

190. Since you only get 24 hours in a day, make them count.

191. Save 2 hours a day, and you give yourself one month each year or 3 months of 8-hour days.

—

192

Some leaders could benefit
from a things-not-to-do list
as well as a things-to-do-list.

—

193.   Priorities are just doing what's the most important.

194.   Everyone says they have priorities, but most don't have a list and live by them.

195.   I know there are a lot of things you can do, but the million-dollar question is should you?

196.   Getting your want-to right is half the battle.

197.   Once you determine your priorities in life, make sure they line up with God's.

198.   You don't have to worry if God can take care of you: He's been doing this for a really long time, and He has tons of references.

199.   The things you can recite at gunpoint are the things that are firmly in your heart.

200.   Major decisions and crazy times don't go together.

201.   Don't believe your own press kit; you are nothing without Jesus.

202.   When you make a mistake and repent, don't get down on yourself. Move on.

203.   You can't control what happens in life, but you can control how you respond to it.

204.   Failure doesn't have to stop you unless you want it to.

205.   Most people forget they haven't always been able to do what they are able to do now. Someone let you sorry all over a group of people and get better. You need to return the favor and believe in others.

206.   Why do some successful people quit dreaming after they are successful? Always schedule time to dream.

" Keeping Life Simple "

Life can sure get wild in the ministry. Have you ever noticed how just when you don't think things can get any busier, they do? We've all been there, but really and truly busy is a relative term. What's busy to me might not be busy to you, and what's manageable to me might be crazy busy to someone else. Whatever your definition of busy is, it is a source of pressure in your life. Pressure is not always bad: it can cause you to grow, or it can expose weakness. The more pressure you are able to handle well, the more responsibility and authority will be handed over to you. The bottom line is our worth to the pastors and churches we serve is tied to our ability to handle the craziness and pressures of life and ministry.

I was forced to delegate. Delegation did not come easy to me. When things would get overwhelming, I would think, I should just find someone to help. But it was hard to let go of things I was good at and enjoyed doing. It wasn't until I moved to Tulsa that I really had no choice but to delegate. When I started working at the church, it was in addition to the job I was already doing traveling and training children's workers. This was before Southwest Airlines™ came along, and in those days, there were cities where a Saturday-night stay was required for the plane ticket to be reasonable. I had no choice but to delegate to others to help me at the church while I was stuck in another state. It was the best thing that could have happened; it forced me to let others help me. Over the years, some of the best lessons I've learned have been from situations I found myself in that made me ask myself, "What am I doing that someone else can do, and what do I need to be doing that only I can do?"

Jesus is our Help and Peace in stressful times. Are you glad you don't have to face life alone when things get complicated? Here's what the Word says in Psalm 46:1, "God is our refuge and strength, an ever-present help in trouble." Not only was Jesus called the Prince of Peace; He is our Prince of Peace. John 14:27 says, "Peace I leave with you; my peace I give you. I do not give to you as the world gives. Do not let your hearts be troubled and do not be afraid." John 14:16 NKJV tells us, "And I will pray the Father, and He will give you another Helper, that He may abide with you forever."

Jesus never leads us into something that will harm us. This Helper or Comforter guides us and leads us to God's perfect plan for our lives. God's plan includes a peaceful life.

Jesus is the Master of simplifying life. The laws of the Old Testament were many and complex, but Jesus made it very easy to follow them:

> *"Teacher, which is the great commandment in the law?"*

> *Jesus said to him, "'You shall love the Lord your God with all your heart, with all your soul, and with all your mind.' This is the first and great commandment. And the second is like it: 'You shall love your neighbor as yourself.' On these two commandments hang all the Law and the Prophets."* —Matthew 22:36-40 NKJV

Jesus' answers concerning life are always simple, even though they may not always be easy to carry out. Paul, too, had a quest to keep life simple. In 2 Corinthians 1:12 KJV, he writes, "For our rejoicing is this, the testimony of our conscience, that in simplicity and godly sincerity, not with fleshly wisdom, but by the grace of God, we have had our conversation in the world, and more abundantly to you-ward." Paul had a heart for following the Lord. He patterned his life after the example of Jesus (see 1 Cor. 11:1). The devil tried to complicate God's simple instructions to Adam and Eve. He still tries today to complicate our lives by injecting thoughts into our minds.

We must choose to keep life simple. It's our choice when things get crazy. Sometimes our responsibilities and the pressures of life affect us in a negative way. We see this in the story of Mary and her sister Martha:

> *As Jesus and his disciples were on their way, He came to a village where a woman named Martha opened her home to Him. She had a sister called*
>
> *Mary, who sat at the Lord's feet listening to what He said. But Martha was distracted by all the preparations that had to be made. She came to Him and asked, "Lord, don't you care that my sister has left me to do the work by myself? Tell her to help me!"*
>
> *"Martha, Martha," the Lord answered, "you are worried and upset about many things, but only one thing is needed. Mary has chosen what is better, and it will not be taken away from her."*
> —Luke 10:38-42

We all are faced with this choice, so to help me keep me on track, here are eighteen steps I use to keep life simple when things are crazy:

1. Set your priorities. You can't keep priorities if you don't have priorities. If you can't name your priorities by number at gunpoint, then they are not how you order your life.

Arrange your events, tasks, and duties by your priorities. My first three priorities never change: my relationship with Christ, my relationship with my family, and my pastor's problems. All

1.

2.

3.

4.

5.

6.

7.

8.

9.

10.

other priorities in my life can change daily. I must be willing to make these choices on a daily basis. Could you make a list right now of your top-ten priorities?

2. *Keep your priorities in order.* As I said above, this is a daily choice. The order of your priorities may be different at times; this is where your leadership must become intentional. My favorite scripture in the whole wide world is Proverbs 28:2, "When a country is rebellious, it has many rulers, but a man of understanding and knowledge maintains order." Maintaining order is the missing element in becoming a super leader.

3. *Delegate to others the tasks they can do for you, even if it's short term.* When you're out of time, use someone else's. There are times I need to delegate something long term; there are times I do it for a season. Make a list of everything you are doing that someone else can do. I hear you saying, "But they can't do it as well as me." I know; I've been there. This is why you use checklists and job descriptions as well as special assignments to get them to do it your way. If you have not identified where you need help and what you need to stop doing, you'll just keep doing what you've always done and have the same results.

4. *Use time-saving tools.* Every job goes smoother when you use the right tools. Here are the tools I rely on to help me keep my life simpler: I have a smart phone (I just try not to do dumb things with it), which happens to be an iPhone™. I also use an iPad mini™ and an Apple Watch™. Each of these has a timer that I use to stay on time and to end meetings, phone calls, and sermons at the exact time I have allotted. I use voicemail, but I try to follow up with either a text or an email, which can eliminate some callbacks and even a meeting or two. (A tip to remember for leaving or sending messages: leave details quickly.) I also depend on the iCloud™ to sync all these devices with the mother ship—my MacBook Air™. I use a laptop because it helps me keep life simple no matter where I go. By having a computer with me everywhere I am, it helps me meet deadlines, network, and brainstorm with others. I can do things once, and through the magic of technology, it all syncs up on my iCal™ calendar. I love being able to share my calendars and invite others to meetings. I depend on several apps such as Todoist™ (it enables me to have a separate to-do list for every project I have, which also allows me to invite others to join). I use a virtual assistant to communicate with my staff called HipChat™. I love Zoom™ for meetings and collaborations. I also use Prezi™ and GroupMe™.

The problem with any of these tools is not letting them become toys; it's all about keeping life simple. I turn off notifications for social media and email, so I don't respond to every ding, and then I only check my devices at specific times each day. I'm also a big fan of WordPress™ websites. Blogs, forums, and websites can be huge assets in communicating with key leaders, workers, and parents.

5. *Do more than one thing at a time.* I try to always make the most of waiting, commute times, and meals. All three of these are great times for study, meetings, people development, time to return messages and emails, to make assignments as well as to plan. I take something to read with me wherever I go. I use a hands-free headset so I can type and check emails while I talk.

6. *Decide what can be postponed or eliminated.* This step goes back to priorities. You are the only one that can determine what's urgent and what can wait. Don't just look at the task; look at the time you have and the time involved. Learn to say no. This is a key skill required to simplify life. I've also learned that a big part of saying yes to urgent and important matters means you MUST say no to less urgent or unimportant things. When time is short, I look to managing me first, others next, and things last.

7. *Get creative with your family time.* I try to take a family member with me every chance I get. I also try to combine my family time with something else. I go walking with Julie, cycling with Julie and Whitney, tennis with Yancy and Julie, movies with my son-in-law, and shopping with them all. I also call them when I can just to say hi.

Helpful Apps:

Todoist™

HipChat™

Zoom™

Prezi™

GroupMe™

8. *Schedule a break, even if it's only for a few hours when you are at your craziest.* Even convicts get time off for good behavior. If I can't go out of town or schedule a massage, I make time to play my guitar, visit a music store, or make a Starbucks or a bicycle store run.. These kinds of breaks are real therapy for me and all take me to a happy place.

9. *Be open to change in your lifestyle.* Different results require different actions.

Don't despise change. Change is not a four-letter word; it's a six-letter word and can be your friend (which is also a six-letter word). When I have to change something that I know is not a permanent change, I remind myself this is only for a short while, and I can do this. As with anything else, guard your thoughts and your tongue, and line them both up with Scripture.

10. *Do your homework, and see what others do in hectic times.* I love to study busy people. I check up on busy people by calling, emailing, reading their books and blogs, and networking at conferences or on Facebook™. I look for new places to learn all the time.

11. *Stop and listen to Jesus.* I shouldn't have to say this to ministers, but make time for the Word! You are the only person who can make sure you stay refreshed and fed spiritually. If you can't go to church, listen to the podcast. Sing and praise God in the car, in the shower, and in the midst of the craziness of life.

12. *When you are tired and busy, don't think: rely on a checklist.* I've been saying this before I got gray hair, "Paper is for remembering, not my brain. I don't try to remember anything that I can know by having information with me."

13. *Don't ever quit or make big decisions during the madness.* Major decisions and crazy times don't go together. This is a key rule to remember.

14. *Don't make people decisions when time is limited.* When it concerns someone else, take your time and consider the situation from every angle. Always treat others the way you would want them to treat you or your kids. Don't let the shortness of the

hour keep you from making a wise decision. Slow things down, and think it through when it affects people.

15. ***Develop a plan to make next year better.*** Learn from your experiences. As soon as an event is over, I ask my team the following: What did we learn? How can we make it better? What do we need to simplify?

Do this while it's fresh on your mind; go ahead and start next year's file.

16. ***Get feedback from others.*** A good leader is a good listener. I consult others beforehand, during, and afterward, so I get a cross-section of opinions from different perspectives.

17. ***When it's over, crash! Get some rest.*** I try to always schedule a break between big pushes. Watch out for too many irons in the fire. Be realistic about the amount of projects you take on. I have learned to get others on board to help limit what I do. I allow others to lead outside projects whenever I can, so I don't take on more than I can handle.

18. ***Do more by doing less.*** Focus on the main thing. Why were you put on the earth? If God has a wonderful plan for your life (and He does), then what is that plan? Focus on your main thing. Focus calls for a concentrated push or intentional actions. What are you doing presently that's keeping you from your main thing? Just because it is a good idea doesn't make it a God idea.

If you are serious about mastering the art of simplifying life, you must master the habit of evaluating constantly. Listen to your spouse. Ask the timeless question, "Where's the beef?" Examine and inspect gains, losses, and fruit. Evaluate efficiency, and look for ways to build systems and streamline efforts. Every experience in your life teaches something. Ask yourself daily, "What did I learn today from life?" and "What should I discontinue, change, and/or add to my life?"

Last but not least, look for your next step. God leads us in steps, not leaps or jumps. We calm the crazy and simplify life by walking life out in steps and then climbing them one at a time.

You can't control what happens in life, but you can control how you respond to it.

CH.

5

"

#STRUCTURE #PLANNING AND #GROWTH

OVERCOMING GROWTH BARRIERS

"

207.
It's always God's plan for anything that's alive to grow.

"

208. The main difference between a growth structure and a maintenance structure is one causes you to go to another level; the other allows you to stay stuck.

209. You don't need the gift of discernment to figure out structure; you need a calculator and good records of your demographics.

210. The right foundation makes the difference in what we build for God.

211. If a hundred new families walked into your church, would you know what to do with them? If not, you have the wrong structure.

212. To become a student of structure means you study other churches, study corporations, and study structure in the Bible. Now ask God what to do, and do exactly what He says.

213. Organizational structure is more than just flowcharts; those tiny boxes on paper need the right person with the right gifts and understanding who operates within the right policies, procedures, and forms.

—

214

Don't get in a hurry.
Anything of value takes
time to build.

—

❝

215.
Just because we don't enjoy waiting on God doesn't mean it's not the right thing to do.

❞

216. A maintenance structure will naturally swallow up your growth structure over time, which is why evaluation is your best friend.

217. To implement your structure, you have to communicate it to your staff, your team, and your whole church constantly.

218. It's not enough to have a plan; you also need to evaluate it and see if it's working.

219. Planning has to go before action.

220. Whatever you don't manage you lose.

221. Your plan is not equal to Scripture, so it's okay to adjust and tweak it. You always know more about a project once you dive in.

222. Life is multi-dimensional. To master a multi-dimensional life, you must learn how to think multi-dimensionally and multitask.

223. Systems naturally get complicated, so you have to be intentional about keeping things simple.

224.	Order + Organization =
Good Management

225.	You don't have to reinvent the wheel every time. Find out what others do, and use selective creativity. (I'm highly selective of whose ideas I rip off.)

226.	Management is the key to promotion.

227.	Managing small things well is an indicator of how you'll handle more.

228.	Six Basic Steps to Organization:

1. Get a vision.

2. Write your goal in steps.

3. Prioritize.

4. Develop a desire to change.

5. Get the right tools.

6. Develop a routine.

229.	We all know that you can pound a nail in with a shoe; but a hammer works better, right? Are you using the right tools for the job you're doing?

230.	The people you delegate to will excel if you understand one principle: people don't do what you expect; they do what you inspect.

231.	Four Steps for Growth:

1. Plan ahead.

2. Think in steps.

3. Evaluate.

4. Delegate.

232.	Any time you delegate without defining how you want it done, the task will develop a weird spirit.

233.	What are you doing that someone else can do? Allow them to do it.

234.	What are you doing that's keeping you from doing what only you can do? Allow someone else to do this for you, so you can do what you need to be doing.

235.	Burnout is never a part of God's plan for any leader.

"

236.
Sometimes knowing what not to do is just as valuable as knowing what to do.

"

237. Always break your responsibilities down into manageable chunks.

238. Organization is the system(s) that causes me to get everything done in my life, and it causes me to be ready for more.

239. Order is putting things where they need to be so they can benefit you.

240. So if God orders our steps, why aren't we asking Him for the next one instead of trying to come up with one on our own?

241. Jesus is the Good Shepherd. We are to be like Him, which means if you're a bad shepherd, stop it!

242. If I can learn from others, then I don't have to make their mistakes.

243. When we've experienced God's faithfulness in small challenges, it helps us to realize that He will be there to help us in the big ones.

244

Rather than sitting back and feeling sorry for yourself, learn to be like David and encourage yourself in the Lord.

245. Quit is a four-letter word; never speak it.

246. Being a learner must be a part of your everyday life if you are serious about growing.

247. Jesus was the master of teaching and encouraging learning by questions. Do you use questions or just ask them?

248. A lot of people aren't willing to take risks to grow. They always worry and say, "What if I fail?" Here's a better question: "What if you succeed?"

249. Learners are not just readers; they are also appliers.

250. One of the main reasons leaders need to continue to grow is so they can help those around them grow.

251. Integrity is more important than talent.

252. Choose to let I don't know move you to I'll find out.

253. A great way to lead change is to apply the Word to every area of your life.

254. Smart work plus hard work always equals success.

255. A growing faith is a questioning faith; there's a big difference between asking questions and doubting.

256. If you want your ministry to grow deeper in the things of the Lord, go there yourself.

257. To lead in ministry, you don't have to be right all the time, but you do need to give up the desire to have people think you're always right.

258. Each change I embrace personally has bettered my ministry and my leadership abilities.

259. If perfection is a requirement, we're all in trouble—especially me; but if you don't aim for perfection, you'll never get better than where you are now.

260. Stop comparing yourself to others; instead compare yourself to Christ Jesus and choose to be like Him.

261. You need to do a checkup from the neck up, and make sure your thoughts are lining up with the Word of God.

262. I can't immediately change others or bring instant change to an organization I am leading, but I can always change me.

263. Learning is not something I have the option of doing: it is a must.

264. It really helps me to depend on God when I admit I don't really know what I'm doing. None of us do!

265. Leaders set the pace for learning in others; followers do what they see leaders do.

266. The intensity of how you pursue exploring and learning is the true sign that sets you apart as a leader.

> 267.
> Don't fall in love with your past successes.

66

268.

I've yet to meet a thankful person who wasn't also happy.

99

269. It takes money to reach people—that's alright because money follows ministry.

270. Challenges will make you grow and will help you be ready for your future.

271. The next time you are facing a lion or a bear, realize that this could be God's way to prepare you for what lies ahead.

272. Everything starts small—that is a biblical principle. But if it stays small, it's time to do a little checkup.

273. Whenever you're shaken, what you've filled your life with is what will come out.

274. Even though you encounter trials and tribulations throughout life, those situations and challenges will cause you to develop character and to produce growth with God if you'll let them.

275. A problem between people is like a problem with plumbing: neither one usually gets better by itself.

276. Problem seasons prepare you for more responsibility.

277. The only people I know who don't have to deal with challenges like stress, budget, and relationships are stretched out in a cemetery.

278. Not everyone alive yesterday woke up this morning. Are you grateful for the opportunities of today?

279. The devil understands that if he can get you to chase good ideas rather than God ideas, then he can keep you running circles; so you will never accomplish the plan God has for your life.

280. Show is needed along with tell. They work better together than on their own.

281. Don't ride a dead horse. I don't care if you go to a seminar on how to ride a dead horse or put more money into dead-horse riding, it just isn't going to work.

282. Every leader's goal is to do right things and do them efficiently.

283. Sometimes in ministry we plan before we pray, but we should stop and pray first.

284. Any change that is not managed will automatically be changed back.

285. Most change will require you to get out of your comfort zone and move away from doing things just like you've always done them, but it will be worth it.

286. People resist change, which is why the change needed is not communicated.

287. The need to change never goes away.

288. Making a great decision doesn't mean much if you present it poorly or at the wrong time.

289. Never be reluctant to ask others to make a commitment; it will take them to a new level of leadership.

290. The most important group that we have to communicate with is the level of leadership directly under us. I learned that from Jesus.

" Overcoming Growth Barriers "

Everyone wants their church or ministry to grow, but they are not always willing to do what it takes. To be perfectly honest, some leaders are more comfortable with old problems and patterns than new solutions. I hear you saying, "Jim, we don't live in the Book of Numbers; we live in the Book of Acts." I agree. Read the Book of Acts, and you'll see it's full of numbers, and they keep getting bigger. God's plan for people and ministries is to start small and then grow.

Being a boy who likes to eat, I've discovered something firsthand. If you buy bigger pants, you'll grow in to them. That's why I do what a lot of Americans do: I have a set size that I will never buy pants bigger than. My options are get arrested for not wearing pants or lose weight. Working at growing churches for almost forty years has taught me to do just the opposite: either grow or do nothing to promote and cause growth. How do I overcome growth barriers? By getting bigger pants. In other words, lay a foundation for growth, and make sure the foundation you establish can handle the growth Jesus wants for you.

The key to any building is the foundation—sound familiar? If you've read my book STRETCH: Structuring Your Ministry for Growth, you've heard that phrase over and over again. The type of foundation determines what you are able to build both in construction and in ministry. This is the reason some churches and ministries don't grow: their structure can't handle it. I classify structure in two main forms: growth structure and maintenance structure. A growth structure will naturally turn into a maintenance structure over time. When I started in ministry, I had seven kids in my children's church. My goal was to hit a hundred, so I structured my ministry for 100 kids. Things were rocking along until I hit about 75 or 80; all of the sudden, I discovered a principle that's still true today: when you are 75 to 80 percent full in a service or room, you are full. Your growth structure just turned into a maintenance structure. It will stay in maintenance mode until it starts to decline, unless you do something to enlarge your structure for your next goal or target. (Same action brings same results.) If you want to grow to 300, you need to enlarge your structure for growth.

There are three main areas that affect growth and that are barriers that keep your ministry small. All three have to be in growth mode to see growth not only happening but also being sustained. The first is organizational structure, which includes policy and procedures. If finding people were no problem, what jobs or careers (as I talk about in my book Volunteers That Stick) do you need to establish? Don't let your need for workers keep you from dreaming. Include middle managers and other coordinators, then answer the questions: what do you want them to do, and how do you want them to do it? Draw up an organizational chart, write the job descriptions, and come up with the policies.

"But that's a lot of work, Jim."

Again, that's another reason folks stay small: they don't want to do the necessary work it takes to overcome growth barriers.

The second main area that has to be in growth mode is people. You need the right people in each of those slots in your growth-mode structure. If you have not read my book Volunteers That Stick, this would be a great time to do so. Reading it is easy; applying what's inside is the hard part. We are not in the program business; we are in the people business. Helping others find their place of ministry and serving is God's plan for the five-fold ministry gifts. Our mission is to prepare God's people for works of service so the body of Christ can be built up.

The third main growth barrier is your facilities. This is why churches build new buildings, start new services, or even go multi-site—to get their facilities in growth mode.

Any one of these three main areas can kick your ministry into maintenance mode. So what are some ways to keep these three areas where they need to be?

1. Have a desire to change; be open to doing whatever it takes. Do what you need to do.

2. Examine your vision and determine the type of structure you need to build. Where do you want to end up? That's all a vision is. Come up with realistic goals for each area, be specific, and make sure this is where your pastor wants you to go.

3. Count the cost. Where are you starting from? Luke 14:28 says, "Suppose one of you wants to build a tower. Won't you first sit down and estimate the cost to see if you have enough money to complete it?" What are the needs? What do you have to work with? What are the strengths?

4. Come up with a plan or a blueprint. Everyone needs a plan. Start with prayer; don't lean on your own understanding. Brainstorm different ideas, and consult a mentor or coach that can help. Always listen to the Holy Spirit, and follow peace.

Lay a foundation for growth, and make sure the foundation you establish can handle the growth Jesus wants for you.

5. Help others know about your plan. Communication is a key to growth. Do the work to communicate, and use every method that you can.

6. Know your team, and always be on the lookout for a new recruit or trade. The best way to do this is by spending time with your team. Watch them in action. Look at things from others' perspectives. Place people by their gifts and abilities. Be willing to make substitutions and include others in the game. Change people's positions if it's best for the team, and always coach folks to their next level.

7. Walk out everything we've talked about here. After everything is done and said, there's always more said than done. Quit having meetings, and work.

8. Communicate upward. Keep the leadership above you in the know and up to date.

9. Communicate laterally. Be a leader's leader. Set the example, and point the way to others. Leave no man or woman behind, which requires setting the right pace.

10. Pursue excellence. Examine the fruit, or ask, "Where's the beef?" You'll never be the best if you don't desire to be the best. Keep updating your own personal definition of excellence. If you aim at nothing, you'll hit it every time.

Here are some important questions to ask yourself if you really want to grow:

Have I established the right structure for what God wants me to build?

Is my present ministry structure a growth structure or a maintenance structure?

Are my present structures, policies, and procedures simple and easy to follow?

Am I committed to doing whatever it takes, even if it means change or doing things I've never done before?

What are you waiting for? You have some work ahead of you, but that's okay. Jesus has only asked us to be obedient to what He tells us to do. He's already promised He will build His church and the gates of hell will not prevail. So, on your mark, get ready, GROW! Dare to overcome your growth barriers.

Every leader's goal is to do right things and do them efficiently.

CH.

6

"

#VOLUNTEERS #PEOPLE AND #WISDOM

STAYING SPIRITUALLY HEALTHY

"

291.
So many ministries I know, especially when it comes to placing volunteers, are like Frankenstein. They've got parts in the wrong places.

"

292. Christians are the only people group I know that confuse the word training with verbal instruction.

293. You can never forget; it's not just about you when you are working on a team.

294. If you had a thousand head of cattle, would you feed them all yourself, or would you get some other people to help you with the feeding process? Church is no different.

295. Give people time off. Remember, even convicts get time off for good behavior.

296. Why should God give you more workers if you're not taking care of the ones you already have?

297. Don't delegate responsibility without also delegating authority.

298. One of the first sermons Jesus preached was about attitude. It's important that you start putting the right heart into those you lead.

—

299

Time is a gift from God.
Treat it that way.

—

"

300.
God never meant for any of us to do the job of ministry alone: it's a team sport.

"

301. Those you lead need to know both your vision and the plan you have to make it come to pass. One tells them where you're going; the other tells them how you're going to get there.

302. Once you duplicate yourself in all areas, then you've got to step back and let people do what you've trained them to do—that's harder than training them.

303. When you instill your heart and passion in another person, you've gone beyond just delegation and have actually duplicated yourself.

304. Delegation is not dumping.

305. Catch people doing things right, and brag on them; it's a great way to lead people.

306. Duplication isn't just your responsibility. Everyone on your team should be a part of the duplication process.

307. Connecting with people to help them use their gifts in serving doesn't happen by accident; it's something you do intentionally.

308. **Ten steps to duplicating yourself in others:**

    1. Identify every position where a worker is needed.

    2. Create job descriptions.

    3. Have a way to discover interests, gifts, and abilities.

    4. Create an organizational structure.

    5. Put your heart into your workers.

    6. Start spending time with the level of leadership directly under you.

    7. Model how you want the job done.

    8. Make assignments and let others work under direct supervision.

    9. Make corrections and adjustments so that it's done your way.

    10. Promote workers and increase responsibilities.

309. **Four great questions to ask yourself about connecting others:**

    1. What areas are you presently over where you need to be duplicating?

    2. What workers do you have now that you see potential in?

    3. What are the key positions where you need depth?

    4. How can you free up and manage your time so that you can start the duplication process in other people?

310. If finding people were no problem, what jobs would you have them do? Take time to dream.

311. I've got some good news for you: you're not supposed to do everything yourself.

312. When it comes to ministry, I should have listened to Three Dog Night: one really is the loneliest number.

"

313.
Never do anything alone. Take someone with you, so you can show him or her how to do what you do.

"

314. There are two types of volunteers: the pigs and the chickens—those who will give you total commitment and those who will just sacrifice. You need both.

315. It is up to you to either stay the same or enlarge yourself and commit to being the kind of person who is consistently enlarging others.

316. Don't be stupid enough to think you can do ministry on your own strength. We're nothing without Him.

317. The first thing Jesus did was use the twelve to establish structure and build something of value. He proves you can't do the workload by yourself. And if the Son of God needed help, you and I need tons of it.

318. Consider it part of your job to be intentional about your relationships with the people God calls into your ministry because it is your job.

319. When everything is said and done, there's usually more said than done. You can fix this if you evaluate.

320

As a rule, good leadership causes increase; bad leadership causes stagnation.

321. As a leader, you set the limit on what sort of helpers your ministry can attract.

322. True servants exist to serve their leaders no matter what their titles or jobs are in the church.

323. God's Word has got to return to being the deciding factor when making choices in all aspects of our lives.

324. It's important to love God's Word more than popular literature or opinion.

325. Want to know if what you are teaching is getting in their hearts? Listen to find out if it's coming out of their mouths.

326. There is a difference in population shift and new birth. God hasn't just called us to have a big crowd: He's called us to go into the world and make disciples.

327. God's Word is the filter through which we should view the world.

328. When we take captive every thought and make it obedient to the Word of God, it produces right thinking that creates right actions.

329. There is a difference between Bible knowledge and a hunger for the Word of God.

330. The Lord can do more through thirty seconds of prayer than we can do in a whole day of preaching. Allow Him to help you.

331. It is not the "sell all you have and move to Africa" messages that we miss. Where we blow it sometimes is missing that still small voice.

332. "Thus saith the Lord" works every time. I have never had to apologize for doing what the Word says: it always works.

333. The Holy Spirit is our Helper, and we must allow Him to help.

334. A great question I like to ask myself on a regular basis: "Has there ever been a time in my life when I was more in love with Jesus than I am right now?" If so, I'm the only one who can fix that.

335. Never forget: we in the ministry are just in sales. God is management.

336. If you spent as much time with your spouse as you spend with Christ, would you still be married?

337. Fear is faith in reverse.

338. Faithful people get where God wants them and stay there no matter what.
They stay plugged in.
They're dependable.

339. A stronghold is believing wrong information; you tear one down by replacing wrong information with the truth of God's Word.

340. In football, you need a second and a third string. Why is ministry any different?

> **"**
>
> 341.
> You're planting the seeds of your own destruction if you don't delegate.
>
> **"**

"

342.

You can't delegate a job you haven't defined.

"

343. There are four words that sum up how to create a volunteer-friendly culture: fun, fair, forgiving, and faithful.

344. If you want volunteers to stick, they've got to know you are forgiving.

345. Recruiting volunteers isn't just about training enough people for the jobs you have open. It's about God calling faithful people into the ministry.

346. I don't want the kids in my ministry to be served by adults who consider volunteering a chore.

347. Career volunteers are people who have a heart for serving others and a desire to use and grow in their skills.

348. It's always better to leave a volunteer spot open than to fill it with the wrong person. Wrong people cost you.

349. Remember, leader, you're building a team and discerning giftedness, not just scribbling names on an organizational chart.

350. Without the right motivation, a volunteer creates way more problems than he or she solves.

351. A little bit of knowledge is a dangerous thing; that's true on a shooting range and it's true in a classroom.

352. My mom has always told me, "What's good for the goose is good for the gander," which is Alabamian for, "Set the example of what you want others to do."

353. Just because you're the leader doesn't mean you have to give an answer right now: it's okay to get back with folks after you've done your homework.

354. To respond involves gathering some information, whereas to react means just letting your emotions decide what to do. Choose to respond to others.

355. I have learned that my job is not to do ministry by myself. My job is to help enlarge those around me to do the work of the ministry.

356. Growth is God's will for all of us.

357. Organization, time management, and leadership are learned behaviors; not everyone is willing to do what it takes to learn them.

358. I'm only married to my wife; everything else is subject to change. (Don't get attached to doing stuff the same way.)

359. All people say that they have priorities, but that doesn't mean they live by them.

360. Sometimes knowing what not to do is just as important as knowing what to do.

361. Communication doesn't just happen on its own; there's a whole lot of work involved to make it happen.

362. In a meeting, there are two things every leader needs to do: they need to watch, and they need to listen, Leaders don't just present information.

363. Leading and communicating go hand in hand: you can't do one without the other.

364. Training isn't just verbal; it's modeling and explaining.

365. When we experience God's faithfulness in small challenges, it helps us to realize that He will be there to help us overcome big challenges.

366. Never be too busy to count your blessings.

367. Communication is a two-way street: there's talking and listening involved.

368. Not only must you intentionally think about communication, you must think innovatively. Don't put all your eggs into one basket.

369. Always communicate with your team before you communicate to the general public.

370. You may not get the whole hog, but that doesn't mean you can't enjoy a ham sandwich. Be thankful for what you have.

371. From time to time, you may place someone in the wrong slot. You need to let people know on the front end that you might need to move them during the leadership journey.

372. Delegation without duplication will not produce fruit that lasts.

373. Set goals that support your priorities, and tweak them until they're specific, measurable, attainable, and time oriented.

374. Lord knows enough things come up that I can't possibly plan for, so I want to plan for those that I can.

"

Staying Spiritually Healthy

"

The key to most of the success in my life is evaluation. Over the years, I've learned that only the things I evaluate will grow and bear fruit. If you were to visit me at any of the churches I've ever served on staff, you'd find me most of the time walking around using my MBWA degree (Management By Walking Around). I spend a lot of time looking at how I spend my time. Each morning I start my day by getting on the scales. When I go to the gym, I always wear a heart-rate monitor. Why? It's simple—one of my goals is for my heart to not jump out of my chest.

All of us rely on gauges to make our lives better. I don't understand what all the gauges do on an airplane, but every time I fly, I am thankful the pilot does. When I get in my car, I check my gas gauge and make sure none of my gauges or warning lights are on. I also believe we should monitor certain gauges in ministry

NOTES:

to keep all of us in leadership spiritually healthy. What's so important about gauges? Let's see what the Bible says in Revelation 11:1 MSG: "I was given a stick for a measuring rod and told, 'Get up and measure God's Temple and Altar and everyone worshiping in it.'" Wow, God was saying evaluate or measure My house, even my most sacred area, as well as everyone who worships there. This is no surprise if you truly believe only the things we evaluate will grow and bear fruit.

Information is power. Gauges let us know what changes or what action needs to take place before it's too late. This is also true about spiritual gauges. Failure or trouble comes from ignoring your gauges. Leaders who ignore their gauges on a regular basis are really not leading; they are only leaders in their minds. You may be asking yourself, "What gauges should a leader be watching in order to stay spiritually healthy?" I'm glad you asked.

The first gauge you should be keeping an eye on is your joy. Some people in ministry become bogged down with to-do lists and tasks, so they forget the secret of their strength—the joy of the Lord. Nehemiah 8:10 says, "For the joy of the Lord is your strength." Growing leaders are joyous leaders. We spend joy every day. It seems like life can be full of things aimed at robbing our joy. Pouty leaders are still leaders. How quickly can you replenish your joy? The silent treatment should never be accepted. You can grow up no matter what your age is. My mom taught me years ago that happiness is a choice. It has nothing to do with your circumstances; it has to do with your thinking as well as your attitude. Don't let your joy gauge or those who lead with you ever get on "E." One of the most valuable skills you can ever develop is to learn how to encourage yourself in the Lord.

The second gauge to keep in check is your attitude. You can't control what happens in life, but you can control how you respond to life. Your attitude is tied to your thinking; that's why wrong thinking produces a wrong attitude every time. Your attitude will make or break you. Philippians 2:5 reminds us our attitude should be the same as Christ Jesus'. Your thankfulness level is also a terrific indicator of your true attitude, and your attitude is a byproduct of your self-image. The key is to line up how you view yourself with what God's Word says about you. When you view yourself according to the Word, it will guarantee you stay spiritually healthy.

The third gauge that will help you stay spiritually healthy is faith. Hebrews 11:6 tells us, "And without faith it is impossible to please God." Wow, I want to please God, so I can never let my faith get low. One of my favorite scriptures is Romans 10:17 KJV, "So then faith cometh by hearing, and hearing by the Word of God." That's really good to know because that is how you increase or build your faith. It comes from hearing God's Word. I have found that one of the best ways for God's Word to get from my head into my heart is by riding the elevator of my mouth. By saying God's Word, it builds my faith. Faith moves you towards the things God wants for you.

The time to build your faith is before trouble comes. That way when you need faith, it's there. First Timothy 6:12 KJV says, "Fight the good fight of the faith." If there is a good fight, then there is a bad fight. You are the only one who can make sure you don't fight the bad fight. To stay spiritually healthy, watch out for the enemies of faith like your feelings or emotions. You can never trust your feelings—ever! An effective leader must master his emotions and keep them to himself in certain times.

Another enemy of faith is fear. My favorite definition for fear is faith in reverse. Fear is the devil's number-one weapon. Everyone's battle with fear is different. No matter what the fear is, deal with it or lose your leadership.

The fourth gauge for spiritual health is the excellence gauge. How is the excellence gauge a spiritual thing? Everything God does, He does with excellence. If you want to do something in a way that will please God, do whatever you do with excellence. Don't settle with aiming at the best when you can aim at the best there is. God tells us in Philippians. 4:8, "Finally, brothers, whatever is true, whatever is noble, whatever is right, whatever is pure, whatever is lovely, whatever is admirable—if anything is excellent or praiseworthy—think

Don't let your joy gauge or those who lead with you ever get on "E."

about such things." When you are pursuing excellence, you'll be spiritually healthy; you'll also be setting yourself up for promotion.

The last gauge I want to encourage you to check is love. The Bible has a lot to say about love; in fact, there are over 680 verses. First Peter 4:8 says, "Above all, love each other deeply, because love covers over a multitude of sins." Love will also move you toward action. John 3:16 tells us that God loved the world so much that He gave His Son. First Corinthians 16:14 tells us to "do everything in love." Love will always lead you in the direction God wants you to go. Love is something that God's people are known for. You can't help but stay spiritually health when love runs supreme. Love will make you a better leader, a better mom or dad, a better boss, and a better employee. It only takes one overlooked gauge to cause a catastrophe in your life and leadership.

If you are serious about being spiritually healthy, you must get in the habit of not just checking these gauges but also feeding your spirit. Remember, ministry looks a whole lot like work. In fact, it is work. Yes, there's a spiritual dynamic; but just like anything else, when you expend something, you have to refill it. A smart leader knows that ministry works in the same way as a checkbook. Make deposits first, then write checks from your overflow.

Here are five ways to keep these gauges on full:

1. *Make an appointment each day to build your faith by having time in the Word.* Set the time for that appointment the day before. It doesn't have to be the same time every day; you just need to treat it like it's special because it is. Don't spend all your time studying the Bible to teach, you have to feed your spirit daily just like you have to feed your body.

2. *Go to church.* I should not have to tell this to people in ministry, but you need to worship and take in from your pastor.

3. *Start every meeting with God stories.* God stories are just reports or testimonies about what God is doing in your ministry. It keeps leaders focused on the main thing being the main thing. If you have no God stories, then things are not very healthy.

4. *Use pre-service prayer as a time to do devotions together or to go through a book as a team.* Don't just read leadership books; find books that challenge you and those who serve with you.

5. *Make time for prayer.* Things happen when you pray. Set aside the time you spend in your car to pray. Put down the cell phone, and pray like it matters. Pray together with your family and with those you lead. When you hem your life with prayer, things are a lot less likely to unravel.

What are your gauges telling you about your spiritual health? Once you identify what you need, then add feet to your plan to fix it.

Above all, love each other deeply, because love covers over a multitude of sins.

1 PET. 4:8

CH.

7

"

#JIMISMS

WHAT OLD JIM WISHES YOUNG JIM KNEW

"

375.
Making a to-do list for tomorrow should always be on today's agenda.

"

376. Innovators and problem solvers will always have a job and be in high demand.

377. Use your lunches to put into people, not just to put food into your belly.

378. When I was in high school, if I had known I would grow up and look like the guy on the chicken bucket, I would have taken better care of myself.

379. The bad thing about the day before a holiday, people are off even when they are working. Don't be one of those people.

380. It's fun to take time off; I should do it more often.

381. Daily thanks-living is more powerful than seasonal thanks-giving.

382. Today I went to a different Starbucks that is closing soon; the staff had lost their joy to serve. It was a good reminder that we should never lose our joy in serving.

383. A great thought for when you have to come back to the church later: if I don't leave, I can't come back.

384

One of the signs of a
kid-friendly church is stepstools
in the men's restrooms.

> **385.**
> Loving people, creating memories for families, and tying those memories to the person of Jesus and His example are what the church should be about.

386. For you who have meetings at Starbucks, if you start getting as many interruptions as you do at the office you may want to find a new hiding place.

387. Even in the church, we reward talent rather than character.

388. The best way for evil to win is for good men to say nothing.

389. Everything we do is a chance to learn and an opportunity that we should take full advantage of.

390. In seasons of unrest, be steady. Our God is the Rock.

391. The thing I like best about not attending a meeting is that I actually get some work done.

392. Some days there are so many people wanting to meet with me I feel like the last biscuit at an all-you-can-eat men's breakfast.

393. Days off are so good; I think everyone

should have one each week.

394. I don't know why we forget as Christians we are all on the same team and need to build the kingdom not us.

395. Systems are like people: they all have strengths and weaknesses. The key is to be willing to make changes and evaluate constantly.

396. Our steps are ordered of the Lord; so if you step into something as a Christ-follower, it's okay. Just keep taking steps.

397. Stay on fire; just don't make an ash out of yourself.

398. I have more to be thankful for than things to complain about.

399. I never get tired of visiting other churches, seeing their facilities, picking up their forms, and going through their closets.

400. I'm practicing one of the secrets of recruiting: I'm attending a service and talking to people before and afterward.

401. A rut is just a grave with the ends blown out.

402. The most effective meetings are short, to the point, or called off.

403. When I was a kid, Burger King had a jingle that said, "Hold the pickles; hold the lettuce; special orders don't upset us." Could that be said of you? I want it to be said of me.

404. There's always a place in my foxhole for can-do people.

405. Better tools help you to be able to do a better job.

406. Had to combine some kids' classes; it's interesting to watch even children resist change.

407. It only takes one overlooked gauge to cause a catastrophe in your life and leadership.

408. I am so proud of my kids. I wish I made the choices they do at their age.

"

409.
The peace of God takes away fear of risks. God's plan is a safe place that always works.

"

410. We were designed by our Creator to rest, so why do we fight it?

411. Every leader needs to know when to stop working.

412. Not every open door is God; listen for His voice before you walk through it.

413. It doesn't matter how you stand when things go well. It matters how you stand when things are difficult.

414. Getting to know the character of God helps you reconnect to the power of God that leads you to cultivate faith in God.

415. Disappointment is an appointment that had a different outcome than what you had imagined.

416. The experiences I encounter each day can always be improved with better leadership.

417. The kindness of a few helps you to overlook the lack of customer service of many, but what would happen if we all just treated others kindly all the time?

—

418

A nurse looking at my chart
that was marked "Recheck Visit"
asked me why I came to the
doctor today. Common sense is
not always common.

—

419. When people realize that Jesus really is alive, they become believers.

420. Each day we have an opportunity to be a blessing and encouragement to others by our attitudes and our actions.

421. I think the next big thing in #kidmin and youth ministry needs to be kids getting excited about living by the Bible.

422. Want to take your life to a new level? Read your Bible, and do what it says.

423. Choose to participate with God rather than be offended.

424. I woke up; it's going to be a good day!

425. For me to lead problem solvers, I must be a problem solver; I must teach and train others to be problem solvers as well.

426. I would rather lead problem solvers than people who just work hard.

427. The Christian life is an open-Book test.

428. Why are you upset about no prayer in schools if you're not praying with your kids at home?

429. It's great to be creative, but why not get creative about caring for people?

430. Lines are a wonderful place to let your light shine for Jesus.

431. Walking out the Gospel is more important than talking about the Gospel.

432. Ever had a project that took longer than you thought it would? It's your choice if it will ruin your day. I choose that it will not.

433. I hated Father's Day as a kid. Why? I didn't have one. Today I love it! God gave me the chance to become the dad I always wanted to have.

434. I love working on Mondays. For seventeen years, I took Mondays off: now I use Monday to reflect about the past weekend and plan for the next one.

435. Looking through the tweets I follow, it is wild how many clowns there are—real clowns, that is.

436. Some days should be spent working on relationships rather than accomplishments.

437. Today I learned the first step in getting things done is standing up. Since then, it's all been downhill.

438. Someone showing confidence in you is a tremendous gift. "I believe in you" are powerful words, so I try to give them often.

439. The moment you quit believing in the people you are leading is the moment you lose the ability to lead them.

440. I love watching the Tour de France with the Mrs. I think I like watching anything with the Mrs. I like watching the Mrs. I am a blessed man!

441. Life is a big game of follow-the-leader.

66

442.

Walking around talking to people and being friendly shouldn't cause you to stick out at church, but it does.

99

66

443.

Heroes in the Bible got there because of the challenges they faced and their choices.

99

444. Seek God, not blessings; and blessings will track you down.

445. What you believe determines your behavior in all things.

446. Once again, I have learned firsthand that most things you dread in your mind are not as bad as you think.

447. Meetings are like guns: they're not inherently bad; it's all in how you use them.

448. Do you want change bad enough to perform different actions?

449. Any opportunity you have to learn is an opportunity you should take advantage of.

450. The worst stuff that happens to you in life is the stuff God will use to promote you.

451. It's more important how you finish than how you start.

452. Had an Australian minister friend ask me today, "Why do so many American pastors

have moral issues?" That's a sad thing to be known for; let's fix it.

453.   Don't be too busy to celebrate the God things that are happening in front of you.

454.   I've dreamed all my life of having the opportunities that are before me now.

455.   When you are frustrated by a group of people, most of the time you are the one who needs to change.

456.   I love Mondays. I also love Tuesdays, Wednesdays, Thursdays, Fridays, and Saturdays; but Sundays are my favorite day of all.

457.   Is Rick Warren really following me or just someone on his staff? In some ways Twitter™ is creepy.

458.   Who you are asking questions to is as important as what you ask.

459.   Friends are the family you choose.

460.   One of the keys of a good meeting is the attitude of those who are in it. I can't control others', but I can make sure I show up with a good attitude.

461.   What fills your mind fuels your passions.

462.   In seasons of great opportunity, there is often great opposition.

463.   Harvest time is visible proof of our God choices.

464.   Church is good; God is better!

465.   When you find a therefore in the Bible, look before it and see what it is there for.

466.   Failure to be thankful on a daily basis is the first step to burnout, moral failure, and selfishness.

467.   At the end of the day, only you can determine if you accomplished the priorities that were necessary—that's why evaluation is vital.

468. Repentance and forgiveness are tools that will help you.

469. Do your workers know how thankful you are for them? You are the only one who can let them know.

470. Pleasure is good, and so is happiness; but joy is better. We should coach others to joy.

471. Finding it easy today to have opportunities to be salt and light. It may be because I'm looking for them.

472. What frustrates me is watching people operate in a bad system and not being able to fix it when, with a little coaching, it would be better.

473. Jesus is more than enough to help us in spite of our poor choices and to help us make good choices.

474. To leave a legacy in the workplace is commendable; to leave a legacy within your family is what God intended.

475. If you could hire someone to take your place, would you look for qualities you have or qualities you want to have?

476. Needing to shut my brain off and stop working. Maybe if I shut my laptop, that would help. I think I'll try it.

477. There is nothing wrong with inviting people to mature and grow up.

478. Leaders get more pushback when dealing with real needs rather than felt needs.

479. You can't give away something you do not have.

480. In seasons of change, leadership is more critical.

481. Remember the people God has put in your life who are for you, not the ones who aren't.

482. If church growth were easy, everyone would be experiencing it.

483

Stubbornness leads to full-out rebellion. The start to flowing with change is staying teachable.

> **"**
>
> # 484.
>
> God has an amazing track record of having man's best interest in mind.
>
> **"**

485.   Just had 1 of the 3 best staff meetings ever. I live for moments when God shows up and opens my eyes to bigger thinking.

486.   Short weeks in the office go better when you practice the fundamentals of time management. Look over your calendar for things you can put off until next week, and set priorities on your to-do lists.

487.   Had to make a serious change in a business relationship today. It's so true—your relationships will make or break you.

488.   Technology is just a tool to get things done. Don't be afraid of new tools for doing old tasks new ways.

489.   I appreciate school crossing guards, but I really appreciate them when the weather is bad.

490.   Just ran into a guy who has been running from God and me for a year. Thank you, Lord, for directing my steps—he heard he was loved.

491.   Talked to a friend that today a year ago was a dark day; today, a year later, it's one of the best ever—only Jesus can do that.

492. Learning should be intentional. It should also be a way of life.

493. If birds of a feather flock together, then what can be said of you by the company you keep?

494. I got so much done today I should write a book on the subject. Oh wait, I did already. #BeatTheClock

495. Look for opportunities to raise your definition of excellence.

496. Willingness is not the standard for whether or not you should take on another commitment.

497. Why not partner with parents the way you would want someone to partner with you?

498. Obedience will always get you to the right place at the right time.

499. Train up a child in the way he should go, and when he is old, he will be in the main service.

500. There is a difference in wanting to know and wanting to learn. Choose to be a learner.

501. A great rule to live by is care about what God cares about.

502. Got out of my car this AM and heard the Lord tell me no new projects. I knew immediately this was right. What's God saying to you?

503. The best principle to pass on to others is the importance of loving others.

504. We are all turtles on a fence post. We would not be there without the help of someone else.

505. Let the things you do and say reflect the Word, and may it produce a desire for children, teens, and adults to become people of God.

" What Old Jim Wishes Young Jim Knew "

A wise old man once told me, "Experience is the best teacher, but it doesn't have to be your experiences that you learn from." Every person I know who is successful has learned from a lifetime of mistakes—theirs as well as the mistakes of others. My mom always told me, "Jim, don't make the same mistake twice; there's enough different ones you can make every time." No truer statement has ever been uttered.

Having done children's ministry in my 20s, 30s, 40s, 50s, and now my 60s; I've had a chance to make a lot of "different" mistakes and choices along the way. Would I do things differently if I could go back and do it again? Sure. I would. We all would because hindsight is always 20/20. Forty years ago, I couldn't have taught you leadership; I hadn't learned it yet. Forty years ago, I had very few workers; I had a big vision but didn't know how to make a plan and lead others; and I was a hard worker but not a smart worker. The good news is God blessed me in spite of myself, but the dreams and vision that were in my heart were not coming to pass. I was smart enough to get some help and do things differently rather than trying to keep doing what was not working while expecting a different outcome. I am so glad that years ago I decided that I would become a lifelong learner. I still am learning, but to do so, I have to just say no to the know-it-all spirit. So with this in mind, here are ten things I wish old Jim could teach young Jim:

1. *Don't be a one-man show; build a team.* When you train, empower, and release others; it releases you to do what only you should be doing. There really is no success without successors. This is a byproduct from team building. Just like in sports, the key to continued success is to build depth at every key position. This doesn't happen by delegation alone but by duplicating yourself and the vision of the house into those you lead. Duplication comes through coaching and hands-on training. Young Jim did it all himself; old Jim allows the team to develop their skills through coaching and encouraging as well as by doing. Everyone does better with a coach.

2. *Watch how you think.* Your thinking controls your actions; it moves you forward or holds you back. I was a lot more opinionated when I was younger than I am now. It took me years before I would and could admit that I don't know what I'm doing. That's why it's always smart to evaluate your thinking and choose to think God's way. I love Philippians 4:8:

"Finally, brothers and sisters, whatever is true, whatever is noble, whatever is right, whatever is pure, whatever is lovely, whatever is admirable—if anything is excellent or praiseworthy—think about such things."

I wish I had done this all the time, but if I'm not evaluating how I think on a regular basis, bad stuff happens. It will always work to your favor to think like Jesus. Think in steps: that's how God leads the righteous.

Think like a parent and those you are serving. Think like a visitor. Old Jim does a lot more checkups from the neck up and takes every thought captive to make it obedient to Christ Jesus.

3. ***Learn from others.*** Read! Join a local Kidmin network. If one doesn't exist in your area, start one. Find a mentor or a coach. (Have you checked out Infuse or kidmincoach.com?) Study those who are successful. Don't just study what they do, but learn why they do what they do. I have come to realize effective leadership is a process, not a pill. Learn the process and the why behind it. Look for a model, but remember to tweak it to fit your church and ministry. Is it wrong to borrow ideas? I sure hope not, or I'd be in trouble. Learn how to copy, but at the same time, learn how to make the copy your own. Ask questions, tons of them, to anyone who will let you. Also never be afraid to try what you are learning—experiment!

4. ***Commit to the long haul.*** Jim, are you telling us when you were younger, you thought about quitting? I sure did—every Monday for a while. It took me a while to stop looking at what I was seeing and have a vision of the finish line. I wish I had known that I shouldn't talk about leaving every time I experienced pushback. I needed to be willing to put my dreams on the backburner to serve someone else's dreams. Every dream I ever had came true by being willing to help others see their dreams come true.

Be secure in your calling. If God called you and is leading your steps, then what you are experiencing, good or bad, is not a surprise to Him. Trust Him to lead you. It's my job to remember leading is all about serving. I've found when I am consumed in better ways to serve kids and families, to serve those who help me, and to serve my pastor; it helps me not be the center of attention.

I'd love to tell young Jim to be on the lookout for fear. Anytime fear is around, you are about to head backwards instead of forwards. Never give into fear; it will always stop you short of the finish line. The two fears that I had to face the most were fear of failure and

Anytime fear is around, you are about to head backwards instead of forwards.

fear of losing my job. You might face different fears; the key is to face them head on and replace fear with faith.

Another enemy of finishing strong is trying to accomplish everything overnight. Too much too quick is always trouble. Do things in phases or steps; learn to live by priorities; have realistic expectations for yourself; and don't stop until you hear God say it's done.

5. *Don't take part in power plays.* I don't know why even as adults we sometimes act like kids. Don't try to get your way all the time. There's no I in team. Old Jim would tell young Jim that thinking about the well-being of others will always lead you to be the team player you need to be. Look for every opportunity to esteem the team. I've never enjoyed being around pouters, so I have to examine myself and make sure I am not pouting. I'd also tell young Jim, there's no place for threats in the workplace. Don't threaten to leave, and don't ever pull out the God-said card in a meeting. If God said it, that's a discussion stopper. Know when you need to lose a battle to win a war. Anytime I enter negotiations, I have to know what I'm willing to give up to take new ground. I've also found that sometimes it's better to keep your mouth shut and not defend yourself so it will not appear like you are arguing. Old Jim knows God is his Defender, and He gives grace to the humble. When it comes to staying away from power plays, don't make someone else look bad to get your way. Old Jim knows that blessed is the peacemaker. Anytime you have the opportunity to make peace, go for it.

6. *Take care of your health.* Old Jim is being forced to do this today. Exercise, sleep, and good nutrition are essential to you being able to finish well. Making time for important things will help you at any age. I wish young Jim knew that making time for exercise has to be a part of your weekly routine, just like meetings and ministry. I know firsthand that all people make time for what they really want to make time for. Old Jim would tell young Jim to make time for the right things. I realize now I have been guilty of working on the wrong temple. Neglecting one to work on the other was not real smart. They both deserve my best, and both need a plan of action.

7. *The law of the lid determines the quality of leaders I can draw.* I didn't realize in my early years of ministry I was holding myself back by not growing my leadership. Go back to number three, and put some action steps in place to improve your leadership level. You will never attack workers sharper than you.

8. *Put your family second only to your relationship to God.* Do things that your family will remember forever. If I could go back in time, I wouldn't spend all my vacation time visiting parents and doing ministry. Guard your days off; make them special for your family. Guard your nights. I think it's important that a family church allows for family time. Listen to your family; be sensitive to their needs. I've found to do this you have to listen with your eyes as well as your ears

9. *Represent your leader well.* Jesus said that if you've seen Me, you've seen the Father. Could this be said of you? Simple things like dressing appropriately, not being silly, not building loyalties to yourself, and never saying negative words about those in leadership above you all reflect on your leader. Be your pastor's biggest fan.

10. *Be a lover of God's people.* The ministry is all about relationships. People matter! I believe the time we spend empowering and encouraging people is never wasted. Old Jim knows people are more valuable than programs, meetings, and study. I'm more thankful for the people God has put into my life than the accomplishments I've seen. People are important to God and should be important to us.

"Finally, brothers and sisters, whatever is true, whatever is noble, whatever is right, whatever is pure, whatever is lovely, whatever is admirable—if anything is excellent or praiseworthy—think about such things."

PHIL. 4:8

#THEEND

T: @jimwideman   F: @jimwidemanministries   I: @jimwideman

Hi I'm Jim Wideman

I never set out to be considered an innovator, a pioneer or one of the fathers of the modern family ministry movement. If you had told me years ago I would get to train hundreds of thousands of children's and student ministry leaders as well as speak to parents around the world, I'd never believed you. Thankfully I was just crazy enough to say yes to Jesus's plan at a young age and now almost 40 years later Jesus is still opening amazing doors of opportunity that I'm just trying to keep going through. Those doors have caused me to become a speaker, teacher, author, and has given me tons of experience in the local church. I love working with parents and helping them see their role as Spiritual provider for their children; I still work in a local church. I'm the Executive Pastor of Northstar Church in Pryor, OK. I also currently serve as an Orange Strategist for the ReThink Group as well as write books, teach leadership, and mentor younger leaders with my Infuse coaching all through Jim Wideman Ministries. But my greatest honor in life is getting to be Julie's husband, Yancy and Whitney's dad, and Sparrow Rocket's "G"!

My prayer is that this book as well as my other books and ministry resources will be a blessing to your life and ministry. If I can help you in any way feel free to contact me at bj@kidmincoach.me.

For more information about my Infuse coaching and mentoring program or a list of all my other books and ministry resources checkout *www.jimwideman.com*

KidminCoach is a place to learn, grow and give. It's a home for theClub leadership resource to have a place to discuss the monthly lessons. It's a home for all Jim's current and past Infusers to stay connected and give back to other kidmin.

This is a place all of us can discuss and study the processes of kidmin. It's where you learn to think like a leader. Why? Because our actions come from our thinking. Effective ministry is a process not a pill!

This Kidmin Leadership Community isn't about being big, or having tons of traffic and stats, it's just a home for learners who have chosen to journey together. While you're there checkout KidminCoach Talk it's like a whole kidmin leadership library all in one blog. So what are you waiting on? Join *Kidmincoach.com* today! If you want to learn more from Jim and those he coaches, *KidminCoach.com* is the place for you.

"

What others are saying about Jim and Tweetable Leadership...

"

"Jim Wideman is not only full of wisdom, experience, and leadership advice — but he is one of the most authentic, genuine, and funny people you will ever meet. Take a look inside the pages of this book and your heart will be filled with all of this — and more."

Adam Duckworth

Lead Communicator - Downtown Harbor Church

Daytona Beach, FL

"Jim Wideman is a leader's leader. God has given him words that inspire and challenge leaders to think bigger. His life back ups everything he says. I'm excited about this new book and recommend you share copies with every leader you know."

Ryan Frank

CEO & Publisher | KidzMatter

Vice President | Awana

"I will always be thankful for the influence Jim had on my early years as a children's pastor. Both then and now, the nuggets of wisdom he graciously shares is impactful and I'm confident this book will be just that – impactful."

Steve Adams

Children's Pastor, Saddleback Church

Jim Wideman is a twitter goldmine. In the years I have known Jim he is amazing at handing out short nuggets of truth when applied will change your ministry. What I love about Jim is he is who he is. He has no filter on his comments and no throttle on his willingness to serve others. I am a better leader today because of Jim's influence in my life. Sit down with a nice cup of sweet tea and read, apply, and grow.

Sam Luce

Campus Pastor, Blogger

Redeemer Church, Utica, NY

"Some people talk about leadership because they see it in others. Jim Wideman talks about leadership because he lives it. Jim is one of the best leaders I know. Jim is forward thinking, innovative, and stays on the cutting edge. I look to Jim Wideman not only to learn about great leadership but also to experience great leadership. I highly recommend Tweetable Leadership to anyone who calls them self a leader."

Matt McKee

Speaker, writer, strategist, pastor and entrepreneur | mattmckee.me

The greatest practical wisdom comes from those who have spent the greatest amount of time in actually doing the ministry. Jim Wideman has never stopped being involved in ministry. Whether he is actively involved in teaching children or coaching those who do, daily he is investing in the lives of others. He is a wealth of wisdom on children's ministries and leadership. This can be seen through the eyes of a multitude of pastors and leaders whose lives have been made better through his influence. I look forward to his next book "Tweetable Leadership" and all it will offer to myself and to others.

David Boyd

National BGMC Director for The Assemblies of God

Jim has been investing in my life for the last 5 years. He's an incredible leader filled with wisdom and experience for you to learn from. Every time I spend time with him I desire to follow Jesus more closely.

I give his books to everyone I know and love sharing his wisdom with others as they try and grow into the leaders that God wants them to become. Buy a copy and another to give to someone worth investing in.

JC Thompson

Student Ministry Pastor

Brookwood Church, Greeneville, SC

I've known Jim Wideman since the late 1970s. Even as a young children's pastor serving down south, Jim's approach to life and the resultant ministry impressed me. Jim is a man of integrity who has modeled the life of a balanced children's leader for decades. I get pumped every time I hear that Jim has produced a new book of leadership helps for the children's minister. Today is no different. I can hardly wait to purchase and read Tweetable Leadership by Jim Wideman. As in everything Jim writes, I am confident it will be packed with practical time and ministry tested truths that will make me a better children's ministry leader. I recommend you open your heart, your ministry, and your wallet to Jim's latest book. You and your church will be glad you made this investment.

Dick Gruber, D.Min

Associate Professor of Children and Family Studies

University of Valley Forge

"I've learned more from Jim about the practical aspects of leading in ministry than any other leader. Every book is ripe with inspirational encouragement, challenging prods and tangible steps you can take to be an effective leader. The prospect of having his most challenging leadership nuggets in a single source called "TWEETABLE LEADERSHIP" is pretty exciting. I look forward to the read."

Gina McClain

Family Pastor Faith Promise Church

Knoxville, TN

CPSIA information can be obtained at www.ICGtesting.com
Printed in the USA
LVOW03s1050210815

450865LV00002B/2/P